P9-DXT-388

SAY IT IN YIDDISH

Edited by
URIEL WEINREICH
Associate Professor of Linguistics and Yiddish Studies
on the Atran Chair, Columbia University

AND

BEATRICE WEINREICH

DOVER PUBLICATIONS, INC.
NEW YORK

Copyright © 1958 by Dover Publications, Inc.
All rights reserved under Pan American and
International Copyright Conventions.

Published in Canada by General Publishing Company, Ltd., 30 Lesmill Road, Don Mills, Toronto,
Ontario.

Standard Book Number: 486-20815-X
Library of Congress Catalog Card Number: 58-11287

Manufactured in the United States of America
Dover Publications, Inc.
180 Varick Street
New York, N.Y. 10014

CONTENTS

INTRODUCTION

SAY IT IN YIDDISH makes available to you in simple usable form the most useful everyday expressions. Translations are idiomatic rather than literal, for your primary goal is to make yourself understood.

PRONUNCIATION

Wherever Yiddish is spoken, different dialects can be heard. This booklet follows the pronunciation of the literary language—i.e. standard Yiddish.

A simplified phonetic transcription is given as an aid to correct pronunciation. The transcription should be read as though it were English with special attention to those sounds marked with an arrow in the table which follows. These sounds have no English equivalents. Stressed syllables are printed in capital letters. Say each word with no break for syllabification. It is not necessary to memorize the table—though you will find it helpful to read through it once. Try to practice some of these phrases—then check yourself with the table. You will find that you have learned this scheme and need refer to it only rarely thereafter. In this phonetic system consistency is sometimes sacrificed for simplicity and ease of comprehension. Listen to native speakers and use this system only as a temporary guide. Don't be too concerned with perfect pronunciation for you can surely achieve comprehension with less than perfect pronunciation.

Unlike English, Yiddish has a regular spelling and each letter is pronounced in a relatively consistent manner. Although Yiddish letters are entirely different from English, they can be mastered in a short time. This accomplishment will not only free you from dependence upon this transcription but will enable you to read signs and names immediately.

SCHEME OF PRONUNCIATION

Letter	Transcription	Example and notes
א		silent
אַ	ah	father
אָ	aw	law
בּ	b	bed
ב	v	vine
ג	g	game (always hard)
ד	d	doll
ה	usually h	house
	(sometimes not pronounced)	
ו	oo	boot
וּ	oo	boot
ו	v	vine
וֹי	oy	boy
ז	z	zeal
ח	kh	ch (guttural, as in the German ach, or the Scottish loch)
ט	t	tell
י	ee	bee
	i	lid
	y	yes (always pronounced as a consonant)
יִ	ee	bee
יֵ	ay	hay
ײַ	i	bite
כ	k	lake
כ	kh	guttural (see ח above)
ך	kh	guttural (see ח above)
ל	l	like
מ	m	me
ם	m	me

7

Letter	Transcription	Example and notes
נ ן	n	*no*
נ ן	n	*no*
ס	s	*so*
ע	e, eh	b*e*d
פ	p	*p*it
פ	f	*f*ee
ף	f	*f*ee
צ	ts	nu*ts*
ץ	ts	nu*ts*
ק	k	la*k*e
ר	r	This sound is different from English *r*. It is formed by letting the tip of the tongue vibrate against the upper gums or by vibrating the uvula audibly (a gargling sound),
ש	sh	*sh*oe
ש ש	s	*s*o
ת	t	*t*ell
ת	s	*s*o

NOTE: In the phonetic transcription *zh* is always-pronounced as the *z* in a*z*ure.

The apostrophe as in SHAW-t'n connotes the absence of a vowel between both consonants. Pronounce like SHAW-tin, quickly slurring over the *i*.

THE INDEX

You will find the extensive index at the end of this book especially helpful. Notice that each entry in the book is numbered and that the index refers you to these numbers as well as page numbers. This indexing method enables you to locate information quickly and without searching the whole page.

THE YIDDISH ALPHABET

The Yiddish alphabet is given below along with the pronunciation of each letter according to the transcription of this book. You will find it useful in spelling out names and addresses.

Letter	Called	Letter	Called
א	SHTOO-mehr AH-lef	כ	khawf
אַ	PAH-sahkh AH-lef	*ך	LAHN-geh khawf
אָ	KAW-mets AH-lef	ל	LAH-med
ב	baze	מ	mem
בֿ	vaze	*ם	SHLAWS-mem
ג	GEE-m'l	נ	noon
ד	DAH-led	*ן	LAHN-geh noon
ה	hay	ס	SAH-mahkh
ו	vawv	ע	AH-yen
ו	meh-LOO-p'm-vaw	פ	pay
וו	tsvay VAW-v'n	פֿ	fay
וי	VAWV-YOOD	*ף	LAHN-geh fay
ז	ZAH-yen	צ	TSAH-dik
ח	khess	*ץ	LAHN-geh TSAH-dik
ט	tess	.	
י	yood	ק	koof
י	KHEE-rik yood	ר	raysh
יי	tsvay YOO-d'n	ש	sheen
יַי	PAH-sahkh tsvay YOO-d'n	שׂ	seen
		ת	tawf
כּ	kawf	תּ	sawf

As you know, Yiddish, like Hebrew, is read from right to left; but our transcription is to be read exactly as if it were English.

*This is the form the preceding letter takes when it appears at the end of a word.

9

USEFUL EXPRESSIONS

1. Yes.
יאָ׃
yaw.

2. No.
ניין׃
nayn.

3. Perhaps.
אפשר׃
EF-shehr.

4. Please.
זײַט אַזוי גוט׃
ZIT ah-zoy GOOT.

5. Excuse me.
זײַט מוחל׃
zit MOY-kh'l.

6. Help me.
העלפֿט מיר׃
HELFT meer.

7. Thanks (very much).
אַ (גרויסן) דאַנק׃
ah (GROY-s'n) DAHNK.

8. You are welcome.
ניטאָ פֿאַר וואָס׃
nee-TAW fahr VAWS.

9. Does anyone here speak English?
צי רעדט דאָ עמעצער ענגליש?
tsee RET daw EH-meh-tsehr ENGG-lish?

10. I speak only English.
איך רעד נאָר ענגליש׃
eekh RED nawr ENGG-lish.

11. I know only a little Yiddish (Hebrew, German).
איך קען נאָר אַ ביסל ייִדיש (העברעיש, דײַטש)׃
eekh KEN nawr ah BEE-s'l YEE-dish (heh-BRAY-ish, DICH).

12. I am a United States citizen.
איך בין אַ בירגער פֿון די פֿאַראייניקטע שטאַטן׃
eekh bin ah BEER-gehr foon dee fah-RAY-nik-teh SHTAH-t'n.

13. I do not understand.

איך פֿאַרשטײ ניט.

eekh fahr-SHTAY nit.

14. Repeat it, please.

חזרט עס איבער, זײט אַזוי גוט.

KHAH-zehrt es EE-behr, ZIT ah-zoy GOOT.

15. Write it down, please.

פֿאַרשרײבט עס, זײט אַזוי גוט.

fahr-SHRIPT es, ZIT ah-zoy GOOT.

16. The address.

דער אַדרעס.

dehr AHD-res.

17. The date.

די דאַטע.

dee DAH-teh.

18. The number.

דער נומער.

dehr NOO-mehr.

19. The time.

די צײט.

dee TSIT.

20. How do you say ——?

װי זאָגט מען ——?

VEE ZAWKT men ——?

21. What is this called in ——?

װי הייסט דאָס אויף ——?

VEE HAYST daws oyf ——?

22. My name is ——.

איך הייס ——.

eekh HAYS ——.

23. I spell my name ——.

מין נאָמען לייגט זיך אויס ——.

min NAW-men LAYKT zikh OYS ——.

24. My mailing address is ——.

מין פּאָסטאַדרעס איז——.

min PAWST-ahd-res iz——.

25. Please speak more slowly.

זײַט אַזױ גוט, רעדט פּאַמעלעכער׃

ZIT ah-zoy GOOT, RET pah-MEH-leh-khehr.

26. What do you wish?

װאָס װאָלט איר געװאָלט?

VAWS vawlt eer geh-VAWLT?

27. Where is (are)?

װאו איז (זײַנען)?

VOO IZ (ZI-nen)?

28. Wait a moment.

װאַרט אַ רגע׃

VAHRT ah REH-geh.

29. How much is it?

װיפֿל קאָסט עס?

VEE-f'l COST es?

30. It is old (new).

עס איז אַלט (נײַ)׃

es iz AHLT (NI).

31. It is (not) all right.

עס איז (ניט) גוט׃

es iz (NIT) GOOT.

32. That is (not) all.

דאָס איז (ניט) אַלץ׃

DAWS IZ (NIT) AHLTS.

33. Why?　　**34. When?**　　**35. How?**

פֿאַר װאָס?　　װען?　　װי אַזױ?

fahr VAWS?　　*VEN?*　　*vee ah-ZOY?*

36. How far?　　**37. How long?**

װי װײַט?　　װי לאַנג?

vee VIT?　　*vee LAHNGG?*

38. Who?
ווער?
vehr?

39. What?
וואָס?
vaws?

40. Here.
דאָ·
daw.

41. There.
דאָרטן·
DOR-t'n.

42. To.
צו·
tsoo.

43. From.
פֿון·
foon.

44. With.
מיט·
MIT.

45. Without.
אָן·
AWN.

46. In.
אין·
in.

47. On.
אויף·
oyf.

48. Near.
נאָענט·
NAW-ent.

49. Far.
ווײַט·
vīt.

50. In front of.
פֿאָר·
FAHR.

51. Behind.
הינטער·
HIN-tehr.

52. Beside.
לעבן·
LEH-b'n.

53. Inside.
אינווייניק·
IN-vay-nik.

54. Outside.
פֿון דרויסן·
foon DROY-s'n.

55. Something.
עפּעס·
EH-pes.

56. Nothing.
גאָרניט·
GOR-nit.

57. Several.
עטלעכע·
ET-leh-kheh.

58. Few.
ווייניק·
VAY-nik.

59. Many.
אַ סך·
ah SAHKH.

60. Enough.
גענוג׃
geh-NOOG.

61. Too much.
צו פֿיל׃
tsoo FEEL.

62. (Much) more, less.
(אַ סך) מער׳ ווייניקער׃
(ah SAHKH) MEHR, VAY-nee-kehr.

63. (A little) more, less.
(אַ ביסל) מער׳ ווייניקער׃
(ah BEE-s'l) MEHR, VAY-nee-kehr.

64. Empty.
פּוסט׃
poost.

65. Full.
פֿול׃
fool.

66. Good.
גוט׃
goot.

67. Better (than).
בעסער (איידער)׃
BEH-sehr (AY-dehr).

68. Best.
בעסט(ער)׃
best(ehr).

69. Bad.
שלעכט׃
shlekht.

70. Worse (than).
ערגער (איידער)׃
EHR-gehr (ay-dehr).

71. Again.
ווידער׃
VEE-dehr.

72. Also.
אויך׃
oykh.

73. Now.
איצט׃
itst.

74. Immediately.
תּיכּף׃
TAY-kef.

75. Soon.
באַלד׃
bahld.

76. As soon as possible.
וואָס גיכער׃
VAWS GEE-khehr.

77. Later.
שפּעטער׃
SHPEH-tehr.

78. Slowly.
פּאַמעלעך׃
pah-MEH-lekh.

79. Slower.
פּאַמעלעכער׃
pah-MEH-leh-khehr.

80. Quickly.

גיך׃

geekh.

81. Faster.

גיכער׃

GEE-khehr.

82. Come here.

קומט אהער׃

Koomt ah-HEHR.

83. Come in.

אַרײַן׃

ah-RIN.

84. It is early.

עס איז פֿרי׃

es iz FREE.

85. It is (too) late.

עס איז (צו) שפּעט׃

es iz (TSOO) SHPET.

86. Men's room.

מענער־צימער׃

MEH-nehr-tsee-mehr.

87. Ladies' room.

פֿרויען־צימער׃

FROY-en-tsee-mehr.

88. I am warm (cold).

מיר איז װאַרעם (קאַלט)׃

meer iz VAH-rem (KAHLT).

89. I am hungry (thirsty, sleepy).

איך בין הונגעריק (דאָרשטיק, שלעפֿעריק)׃

eekh bin HOON-geh-rik (DOR-shtik, SHLEH-feh-rik).

90. I am (not) in a hurry.

איך אײל זיך (ניט)׃

eekh IL zikh (nit).

91. I am busy (tired, ill).

איך בין פֿאַרנומען (מיד, קראַנק)׃

eekh bin fahr-NOO-men (MEED, KRAHNK).

92. I am lost.

איך האָב פֿאַרבלאָנדזשעט׃

eekh hawb fahr-BLAWN-jet.

93. I am looking for ——.

איך זוך ——׃

eekh ZOOKH ——.

94. I am glad.   **I am sorry.**

איך בין צופֿרידן.   עס פֿאַרדריסט מיר.

eekh bin tsoo-FREE-d'n.   *es fahr-DREEST meer.*

95. I am ready.

איך בין גרייט.

eekh bin GRAYT.

96. Can you tell me?

צי קענט איר מיר זאָגן?

tsee KENT eer meer ZAW-g'n?

97. What is that?

וואָס איז דאָס?

VAWS iz DAWS?

98. I should like.

איך וואָלט געוואָלט.

eekh vawlt geh-VAWLT.

99. Can you recommend ——?

צי קענט איר רעקאָמענדירן ——?

tsee KENT eer reh-kaw-men-DEE-r'n ——?

100. Do you want ——?

צי ווילט איר ——?

tsee VILT eer ——?

101. I (do not) know.

איך ווייס (ניט).

eekh VAYS (nit).

102. I think so.

אַזוי מיין איך.

ah-ZOY MAYN eekh.

DIFFICULTIES

103. I cannot find my hotel address.

איך קען ניט געפֿינען דעם אַדרעס פֿון מײַן
האָטעל.

*eekh KEN nit geh-FEE-nen dem AHD-res foon mĭn
haw-TELL.*

104. I do not remember the street.

איך געדענק ניט די גאַס.

eekh geh-DENK nit dee GAHS.

105. I have lost my friends.

איך האָב פֿאַרלוירן מײַנע פֿרײַנד.

eekh hawb fahr-LOY-r'n mĭ-neh FRIND.

106. I left my purse (wallet) in the ——.

איך האָב איבערגעלאָזט מײַן בײַטל (בײַטעלע)
אין ——.

*eekh hawb EE-behr-geh-lawst mĭn BĬ-t'l (BĬ-teh-leh)
in ——.*

107. I forgot my money (my keys).

איך האָב פֿאַרגעסן מײַן געלט (מײַנע שליסל).

*eekh hawb fahr-GEH-s'n mĭn GELT (mĭ-neh SHLEE-
s'l).*

108. I have missed my train (the plane, the bus).

איך האָב פֿאַרזאָמט די באַן (דעם אַעראָפּלאַן,
דעם אויטאָבוס).

*eekh hawb fahr-ZAMT dee BAHN (dem ah-eh-rawp-
LAHN, dem oy-taw-BOOS).*

109. What is the matter here?

וואָס איז דאָ דער מער?

VAWS iz daw dehr MEHR?

110. What am I to do?

וואָס דאַרף איך טאָן?

VAWS dahrf eekh TAWN?

111. It is (not) my fault.

איך בין (ניט) שולדיק.

EEKH bin (nit) SHOOL-dik.

112. They are bothering me.

זיי טשעפּען זיך צו מיר.

zay CHEH-pen zikh tsoo meer.

113. Go away.

גייט אַוועק.

GAYT ah-VEK.

114. I will call a policeman.

איך וועל רופֿן אַ פּאָליציאַנט.

eekh vel ROO-fn ah paw-lits-YAHNT.

115. Where is the police station?

וואו איז די פּאָליציי־סטאַנציע?

VOO iz dee paw-lee-TSAY-stahnts-yeh?

116. I have been robbed of ——.

מען האָט בײַ מיר צוגעגנבֿעט ——.

men hawt bī meer TSOO-geh-gahn-vet ——.

117. The lost and found desk.

דאָס ביוראָ פֿאַר געפֿונענע זאַכן.

daws bew-RAW fahr geh-FOO-neh-neh ZAH-kh'n.

118. Help!

געוואַלד!

geh-VAHLD!

119. Fire!

עס ברענט!

es BRENT!

120. Thief!

גנבֿ!

GAH-nev!

121. Look out!

היט זיך!

HEET zikh!

122. Stop!

אויפֿהערן!

OYF-hehrn!

123. Listen!

הערט!

hehrt!

GREETINGS AND SOCIAL CONVERSATION

124. Good morning.
גוט מאָרגן׃

goot MOR-g'n.

125. Good evening.
גוטן אָוונט׃

GOO-t'n AW-v'nt.

126. Hello (Good Sabbath).
שלום-עליכם (גוט שבת)׃

SHAW-lem ah-LAY-khem (goot SHAH-bes).

127. Good-bye.
אַ גוטן טאָג׃

ah GOO-t'n TAWG.

128. I'll be seeing you.
זײט מיר דערװײל געזונט׃

ZIT meer dehr-VIL geh-ZOONT.

129. What is your name?
װי הייסט איר?

vee HAYST eer?

130. May I introduce Mr. (Mrs., Miss) ——?
צי קען איך אײך פֿאָרשטעלן הער (פֿרוי,
פֿרײלין) ——?

*tsee KEN eekh ĭkh FOR-shteh-l'n hehr (froy, frĭ-l'n)
——?*

131. My wife.
מײן פֿרוי׃

mĭn FROY.

132. My husband.
מײן מאַן׃

mĭn MAHN.

133. My daughter.
מײן טאָכטער׃

mĭn TAWKH-tehr.

134. My son.
מײן זון׃

mĭn ZOON.

135. My mother.
מײַן מאַמע׃

mĭn MAH-meh.

136. My father.
מײן טאַטע׃

mĭn TAH-teh.

137. My friend.
מײַן פֿרײַנד.
mîn FRIND.

138. My relative.
מײַן קרוב (or) קרובֿה.
mîn KAW-rev or
KROY-veh.

139. My grandmother.
מײַן באַבע.
mîn BAW-beh.

140. My grandfather.
מײַן זיידע.
mîn ZAY-deh.

141. My sister.
מײַן שוועסטער.
mîn SHVES-tehr.

142. My brother.
מײַן ברודער.
mîn BROO-dehr.

143. I am a friend of Mr. ——.
איך בין הער ——ס אַ פֿרײַנד.
eekh bin hehr ——s ah FRIND.

144. I am happy to make your acquaintance.
עס פֿרייט מיך איך צו קענען.
es FRAYT mikh îkh tsoo KEH-nen.

145. How are you?
וואָס מאַכט איר?
vaws MAHKHT eer?

146. Fine, thanks. And you?
גוט, אַ דאַנק. און איר?
GOOT, ah DAHNK. oon EER?

147. How is your family?
וואָס מאַכט אײַער משפּחה?
vaws MAHKHT î-ehr mish-PAW-kheh?

148. (Not) very well.
(ניט) זייער גוט.
(NIT) zay-ehr GOOT.

149. Sit down, please.
זעצט זיך אַוועק, זיט אַזוי גוט.
ZETST zikh ah-VEK, zît ah-zoy GOOT.

150. I have enjoyed myself very much.

איך האָב זייער גוט פֿאַרבראַכט׃

eekh hawb ZAY-ehr GOOT fahr-BRAHKT.

151. I hope to see you again soon.

איך האָף אַז מיר וועלן זיך באַלד ווידער זען׃

*eekh HAWF ahz meer veh-l'n zikh BAHLD VEE-dehr
ZEN.*

152. Come to see me (us).

קומט צו מיר (אונדז)׃

KOOMT tsoo MEER (OONDZ).

**153. Give me your address (and telephone num-
ber).**

גיט מיר אייער אַדרעס (און טעלעפֿאָן־נומער)׃

*GEET meer ī-ehr AHD-res (oon teh-leh-FAWN-noo-
mehr).*

154. My regards to your family.

אַ גרוס אייער משפּחה׃

ah GROOS ī-ehr mish-PAW-kheh.

155. We are traveling to ——.

מיר פֿאָרן קיין ——׃

meer FAW-r'n kayn ——.

156. Congratulations.

מזל־טובֿ׃

MAH-z'l-tawv.

157. Happy Birthday.

מזל־טובֿ צום געבוירן־טאָג׃

MAH-z'l-tawv tsoom geh-BOY-r'n-tawg.

158. Happy New Year.

אַ גוט יאָר׃

ah GOOT YAWR.

159. Happy Holiday (Good Sabbath).

גוט יום־טוב (גוט שבת)·

goot YAWN-tev (goot SHAH-bes).

TRAVEL: GENERAL EXPRESSIONS

160. Can you direct me to a travel agency (an airline office)?

צי קענט איר מיר זאָגן װאו עס געפֿינט זיך אַ
רײַזע־ביוראָ (אַ לופֿטליניע־ביוראָ)?

tsee KENT eer meer ZAW-g'n VOO es geh-FINT zikh
ah RI-zeh-bew-raw (ah LOOFT-lin-yeh-bew-raw)?

161. I want to go to the airport (the bus station, the street car).

איך װיל צוקומען צום פֿליפֿלאַץ (צו דער
אויטאָבוס־סטאַנציע, צום טראַמװײ)·

ikh vil TSOO-koo-men tsoom FLEE-plahts (tsoo dehr
oy-taw-BOOS-stahnts-yeh, tsoom trahm-VI).

162. Is the railroad station (bus depot) near here?

צי איז דער װאָקזאַל (די אויטאָבוס־סטאַנציע)
נאָענט פֿון דאַנען?

tsee iz dehr vawk-ZAHL (dee oy-taw-BOOS-stahnts-
yeh) NAW-ent foon DAH-nen?

163. The car fare.

דאָס פֿאָרגעלט·

daws FOR-gelt.

164. The transfer.

דער טראַנספֿעריר־בילעט·

dehr trahns-feh-REER-bee-let.

165. The subway token.

די סאבװײ־מטבע·

dee SUB-vay-maht-BAY-eh.

166. The commutation ticket.

דער אבאָנעמענט־בילעט.

dehr ah-baw-neh-MENT-bee-let.

167. What is the best way of traveling?

ווי פֿאָרט מען צום בעסטן?

VEE FORT men tsoom BES-t'n?

168. How long will it take to go to ——?

ווי לאַנג פֿאָרט מען ביז ——?

VEE LAHNGG FORT men biz ——?

169. When will we arrive at ——?

ווען וועלן מיר אָנקומען אין ——?

VEN veh-l'n meer AWN-koo-men in ——?

170. Please get me a taxi.

זײַט אַזוי גוט, קריגט מיר אַ טאַקסי.

ZIT ah-zoy GOOT, KRIGT meer ah TAHK-see.

171. Where is the baggage room?

וואו איז דער באַגאַש־צימער?

VOO iz dehr bah-GAHZH-tsee-mehr?

172. I need a porter.

איך דאַרף אַ טרעגער.

eekh DARF ah TREH-gehr.

173. Follow me please.

זײַט אַזוי גוט, גייט מיר נאָך.

ZIT ah-zoy GOOT, GAYT meer NAWKH.

174. Can I reserve a (front) seat?

צי קען איך רעזערווירן אַ זיצאָרט (פֿון פֿאָרנט)?

tsee KEN eekh reh-zehr-VEE-r'n ah ZITS-ort (foon FAW-r'nt)?

175. I want a seat near the window.

איך וויל אַן אָרט לעבן פֿענצטער.

eekh VIL ahn ORT leh-b'n FENTS-tehr.

176. Is this seat taken?

צי איז דער אָרט פֿאַרנומען?

tsee iz dehr ORT fahr-NOO-men?

177. Where is the nearest station?

וואו איז די נאָענטסטע סטאַנציע?

VOO iz dee NAW-ents-teh STAHNTS-yeh?

178. Is this the (direct) way to ——?

צי איז דאָס דער (דירעקטער) וועג קיין ——?

tsee iz DAWS dehr (dee-REK-tehr) VEG kayn ——?

179. Which is quicker?

וועלכער איז גיכער?

VEL-khehr iz GEE-khehr?

180. How does one go (there)?

ווי אַזוי פֿאָרט מען (אַהין)?

vee ah-ZOY FORT men (ah-HEEN)?

181. Show me on the map.

ווײַזט מיר אויף דער קאַרטע.

VIST meer oyf dehr KAR-teh.

182. Does it stop at ——?

צי שטעלט זיך עס אָפּ אין ——?

tsee SHTELT zikh es AWP in ——?

183. Where do I turn?

וואו זאָל איך זיך פֿאַרקערעווען?

VOO zawl eekh zikh fahr-KEH-reh-ven?

184. To the north.

אויף צפֿון.

oyf TSAW-f'n.

185. To the south.

אויף דרום.

oyf DAW-rem.

186. To the east.

אויף מיזרח.

oyf MIZ-rahkh.

187. To the west.

אויף מערב.

oyf MI-rev.

188. To the right.
·אויף רעכטס·
oyf REKHTS.

189. To the left.
·אויף לינקס·
oyf LINKS.

190. Straight ahead.
·גליך·
glikh.

191. Corner.
·ראָג·
rawg.

192. Forward.
·פֿאָרויס·
faw-ROYS.

193. Back.
·צוריק·
tsoo-RIK.

194. Street.
·גאַס·
gahs.

195. Circle.
·קײלעכדיקער פּלאַץ·
KĪ-lekh-dee-kehr
    PLAHTS.

196. Place.
·פּלאַץ·
plahts.

197. Avenue.
·עוועניו·
EH-veh-new.

198. Square.
·סקווער·
skvehr.

199. Park.
·פּאַרק·
pahrk.

200. Am I going in the right direction?
צי גיי איך אין דער ריכטיקער ריכטונג?
tsee GAY eekh in dehr REEKH-tee-kehr REEKH-
    toongg?

201. Please point.
·זיט אַזוי גוט· וויזט אָן·
ZIT ah-zoy GOOT, VIST AWN.

202. What street is this?
וואָסער גאַס איז דאָס?
VAW-sehr GAHS iz DAWS?

203. Do I have to change?

צי דאַרף איך זיך איבערזעצ'ן?

tsee DAHRF eekh zikh EE-behr-zeh-ts'n?

204. Please tell me where to get off.

זײַט אַזוי גוט, זאָגט מיר וואו אַראָפּצוגיין•

ZIT ah-zoy GOOT, ZAWKT meer VOO ah-RAWP-tsoo-gayn.

TICKETS AND TRAIN

205. Where is the ticket office?

וואו איז די קאַסע?

VOO iz dee KAH-seh?

206. I need a ticket to ——.

איך דאַרף אַ בילעט קיין ——•

eekh DAHRF ah bee-LET kayn ——

207. A timetable.

אַ פֿאָרפּלאַן•

ah FAWR-plahn.

208. How much is a one-way (a round trip) ticket to ——?

וויפֿל קאָסט אַ בילעט אין איין ריכטונג (אַהין
און צוריק) קיין ——?

VEE-f'l COST ah bee-LET in AYN REEKH-toongg (ah-HEEN oon tsoo-RIK) kayn ——?

209. First (second, third) class.

ערשטע (צווייטע, דריטע) קלאַס•

EHR-shteh (TSVAY-teh, DRIT-eh) KLAHS.

210. Is there an express (a local) train to ——?

צי איז פֿאַראַן אַן עקספּרעס־ (אַ לאָקאַל־) צוג
קיין ——?

tsee iz fah-RAHN ahn ex-PRES- (ah law-KAHL-) tsoog kayn ——?

211. A reserved seat.

אַ רעזערווירטער זיצאָרט·

ah reh-zehr-VEER-tehr ZITS-ort.

212. Can I go by way of ——?

צי קען איך פֿאָרן דורך ——?

tsee KEN eekh FAW-r'n doorkh ——?

213. Is there a later (an earlier) train?

צי איז פֿאָראַן אַ צוג שפּעטער (פֿריִער)?

tsee iz fah-RAHN ah TSOOG SHPEH-tehr (FREE-ehr)?

214. From what station (gate, track) do I leave?

פֿון וועלכן וואָקזאַל (טויער, פּעראָן) פֿאָר איך אָפּ?

foon VEL-kh'n vawk-ZAHL (TOY-ehr, peh-RAWN) FAWR eekh AWP?

215. How long is this ticket good?

אויף ווי לאַנג איז גילטיק דער בילעט?

oyf VEE LAHNGG eez GIL-tik dehr bee-LET?

216. Can I get something to eat on the way?

צי קען איך קריגן עפּעס צו עסן אונטער וועגנס?

tsee KEN eekh KRIG'n eh-pes tsoo EH-s'n oon-tehr VEH-g'ns?

217. How much baggage may I take?

וויפֿל באַגאַזש מעג איך מיטנעמען?

VEE-f'l bah-GAHZH meg eekh MIT-neh-men?

CUSTOMS

218. Where is the customs?

וואו איז דער צאָלאַמט?

VOO iz dehr TSAWL-ahmt?

219. Here is my baggage, three pieces.

אָט איז מײַן באַגאַזש, דרײַ שטיק׃

AWT iz min bah-GAHZH, drĭ SHTEEK.

220. This package contains clothing (food, books).

אין דעם פּעקל ליגן קליידער (עסנוואַרג, ביכער)׃

in dem PEH-k'l LIG'n KLAY-dehr (EH-s'n-vahrg, BEE-khehr).

221. Here is my passport (my visa).

אָט איז מײַן פּאַס (מײַן וויזע)׃

AWT iz min PAHS (mĭn VEE-zeh).

222. I have my landing ticket.

איך האָב די דערלויבעניש אַראָפּצוגיין פֿון דער שיף׃

eekh HAWB dee dehr-LOY-beh-nish ah-RAWP-tsoo-gayn foon dehr SHIF.

223. I am a tourist on vacation.

איך בין אַ טוריסט אויף וואַקאַציע׃

eekh bin ah too-RIST oyf vah-KAHTS-yeh.

224. Are you a new American?

צי זײַט איר אַ נײַער אַמעריקאַנער?

tsee ZIT eer ah NAH-yehr ah-meh-ree-KAH-nehr?

225. This is a business visit.

דאָס איז אַ געשעפֿטלעכער באַזוך׃

daws iz ah geh-SHEFT-leh-kehr bah-ZOOKH.

226. I am in transit.

איך האַלט אין דורכפֿאָרן׃

eekh HAHLT in DOORKH-faw-r'n.

227. Must I open everything?

צי מוז איך אַלץ עפֿענען?

tsee MOOZ eekh AHLTS EH-feh-nen?

228. I cannot open that.

דאָס קען איך ניט עפֿענען.

DAWS KEN eekh nit EH-feh-nen.

229. I have nothing to declare.

איך האָב ניט װאָס צו דעקלאַרירן.

eekh HAWB nit VAWS tsoo deh-klah-REE-r'n.

230. All this is for my personal use.

דאָס אַלץ איז פֿאַר מײן אײגענעם באַנוץ.

daws AHLTS iz fahr mīn AY-geh-nem bah-NOOTS.

231. There is nothing here but ——.

עס איז דאָ קײן זאַך ניט פֿאַראַן אַחוץ ——.

es iz daw KAYN zahkh nit fah-RAHN ah-KHOOTS ——.

232. These are gifts.

דאָס זײנען מתנות.

DAWS zī-nen mah-TAW-nes.

233. Are these things dutiable?

צי קומט אױף די זאַכן צאָל?

tsee KOOMT oyf DEE ZAH-kh'n TSAWL?

234. How much must I pay?

װיפֿל דאַרף איך צאָלן?

VEE-f'l DAHRF eekh TSAW-l'n?

235. This is all I have.

מער װי דאָס האָב איך ניט.

MEHR vee DAWS HAWB eekh nit.

236. Please be careful.

זײט אַזױ גוט, זײט אָפּגעהיט.

ZIT ah-zoy GOOT, ZIT AWP-geh-heet.

237. Have you finished?

צי האָט איר געענדיקט?

tsee hawt eer geh-EN-dikt?

238. I cannot find all my baggage.

איך קען ניט געפֿינען מיין גאַנצן באַגאַזש·

eekh KEN nit geh-FEE-nen min GAHN-ts'n bah-GAHZH.

239. My train leaves in —— minutes.

מיין באַן פֿאָרט אָפּ אין —— מינוט אַרום·

min BAHN fort AWP in —— mee-NOOT ah-ROOM.

BAGGAGE

240. Where is the baggage checked?

וואו גיט מען אָפּ דעם באַגאַזש?

VOO git men AWP dem bah-GAHZH?

241. I want to leave these bags for a while.

איך וויל איבערלאָזן די טשעמאָדאַנעס אויף
אַ ווײלע·

eekh vil EE-behr-law-z'n dee cheh-maw-DAH-nes oyf ah VI-leh.

242. Do I pay now or later?

צי דאַרף איך צאָלן איצט צי שפּעטער?

tsee dahrf eekh TSAW-l'n ITST tsee SHPEH-tehr?

243. I want to take out my baggage.

איך וויל אַרויסנעמען מיין באַגאַזש·

eekh vil ah-ROYS-neh-men min bah-GAHZH.

244. That is mine over there.

יענער איז מײנער אָט דאָרטן·

YEH-nehr iz MI-nehr awt DOR-t'n.

245. Handle this very carefully.

באַגייט זיך זייער פֿאָרזיכטיק מיט דעם·

bah-GAYT zikh ZAY-ehr FOR-zikh-tik mit dem.

246. Where can I find the station master?

װאו קען איך געפֿינען דעם װאָקזאַל־פֿאַרװאַל־
טער?

VOO ken eekh geh-FIN-en dem vawk-ZAHL-fahr-vahl-tehr?

AIRPLANE

247. Is there bus service to the airport?

צי איז פֿאַראַן אַן אױטאָבוס־דינסט צום
פֿליפּלאַץ?

tsee iz fah-RAHN ahn oy-taw-BOOS-deenst tsoom FLEE-plahts?

248. At what time will they come for me?

װיפֿל אַ זײגער װעט מען מיך אָפּנעמען?

VEE-f'l ah-ZAY-gehr vet men mikh AWP-neh-men?

249. When is there a plane to ——?

װען גייט אַן אעראָפּלאַן קײן ——?

VEN gayt ahn ah-eh-rawp-LAHN kayn ——?

250. What is the flight number?

װי איז דער נומער פֿון קורס?

VEE iz dehr NOO-mehr foon KOORS?

251. Is food served on the plane?

צי גיט מען עסן אין אעראָפּלאַן?

tsee GIT men EH-s'n in ah-eh-rawp-LAHN?

252. How many kilos may I take?

װיפֿל קילאָ מעג איך מיטנעמען?

VEE-f'l KEE-law meg eekh MIT-neh-men?

253. How much per pound for excess?

װיפֿל קאָסט יעדער איבעריקער פֿונט?

VEE-f'l COST YEH-dehr EE-beh-ree-kehr FOONT?

BOAT

254. Can I go by boat (ferry) to ——?

צי קען איך פֿאָר׳ן מיט אַ שיף (פֿאַראָם) קיין ——?

*tsee KEN eekh FAW-r'n mit ah SHIF (pah-RAWM)
kayn ——?*

255. When does the next boat leave?

ווען גייט אַפּ די קומענדיקע שיף?

VEN gayt AWP dee KOO-men-dee-keh SHIF?

256. When must I go on board?

ווען מוז איך אַרויף אויף דער שיף?

VEN mooz eekh ah-ROYF oyf dehr SHIF?

257. Can I land at ——?

צי קען איך אַראָפּגיין אין ——?

tsee KEN eekh ah-RAWP-gayn in ——?

258. The captain.

דער קאַפּיטאַן•

dehr kah-pee-TAHN

259. The officer.

דער אָפֿיציר•

dehr aw-fee-TSEER.

260. The deck.

דער דעק•

dehr DECK.

261. Upper.

אייבערשטער•

AY-behrsh-tehr.

262. Lower.

אונטערשטער•

OON-tehrsh-tehr.

263. Where can I find the purser (the steward)?

וואו קען איך געפֿינען דעם שיף־קאַסירער (דעם סטוואַרד)?

*VOO ken eekh geh-FIN-en dem SHIF-kah-see-rehr
(dem STEW-ahrd)?*

264. I want to rent a deck chair.

איך וויל דינגען אַ דעקשטול•

eekh vil DIN-gen ah DECK-shtool.

265. I am seasick.

איך בין ים־קראנק·

eekh bin YAHM-krahnk.

266. Please prepare my berth.

זײַט אַזױ גוט, גרייט צו מײַן בעט·

ZIT ah-zoy GOOT, GRAYT TSOO mīn BET.

267. I am going to my stateroom.

איך גיי אין מײַן קאַיוטע·

eekh GAY in mīn kah-YOO-teh.

268. Let's go to the dining room.

לאָמיר גיין אין עסזאַל·

LAW-meer GAYN in ES-zahl.

269. A life boat.

אַ ראַטירשיפֿל·

ah rah-TEER-shee-f'l.

270. A life preserver.

אַ ראַטיררינג·

ah rah-TEER-ringg.

BUS

271. Where is the bus station?

װאו איז די אױטאָבוס־סטאַנציע?

VOO iz dee oy-taw-BOOS-stahnts-yeh?

272. Can I buy an excursion ticket?

צי קען איך קױפֿן אַן עקסקורסיע־בילעט?

tsee KEN eekh KOY-f'n ahn ex-KOORS-yeh-bee-lei?

273. Is there a stop for lunch?

צי שטעלט מען זיך אָפּ אױף מיטאָג?

tsee SHTELT men zikh AWP oyf MIT-awg?

274. May I stop on the way?

צי קען איך זיך אָפּשטעלן אונטער װעגנס?

tsee KEN eekh zikh AWP-shteh-l'n oon-tehr VEH-g'ns?

CITY BUS, STREETCAR AND SUBWAY

275. What bus (street car) do I take?
וואָסער אויטאָבוס (טראַמוויי) זאָל איך נעמען?

VAW-sehr oy-taw-BOOS (trahm-VĪ) zawl eekh NEH-men?

276. Is there a subway?
צי איז פֿאַראַן אַ סאַבוויי (אונטערבאַן)?

tsee iz fah-RAHN ah SUB-way (OON-tehr-bahn)?

277. How much is the fare?
וויפֿל באַטרעפֿט דאָס פֿאָרגעלט?

VEE-f'l bah-TREFT daws FOR-gelt?

278. Where does the bus for —— stop?
וואו שטעלט זיך אָפּ דער אויטאָבוס קיין ——?

VOO SHTELT zikh AWP dehr oy-taw-BOOS kayn ——?

279. The bus stop.
דער אויטאָבוס־אָפּשטעל.

dehr oy-taw-BOOS-awp-shtel.

280. The driver.
דער שאָפֿער.

dehr shaw-FEHR.

281. Do you go near ——?
צי פֿאָרט איר לעבן ——?

tsee FORT eer LEH-b'n ——?

282. A transfer, please.
אַ טראַנספֿעריר־בילעט, זײַט אַזױ גוט.

ah trahns-feh-REER-bee-let, ZĪT ah-zoy GOOT.

283. I want to get off at the next stop.
איך וויל אַראָפּגײן בײַם קומענדיקן אָפּשטעל.

eekh VIL ah-RAWP-gayn bīm KOO-men-dee-k'n AWP-shtel.

TAXI

284. Please call a taxi for me.

זײַט אַזױ גוט, רופֿט מיר אַ טאַקסי.

ZIT ah-zoy GOOT, ROOFT meer ah TAHK-see.

285. How far is it?

װי װײַט איז עס?

VEE VIT iz es?

286. How much will it cost?

װיפֿל װעט עס קאָסטן?

VEE-f'l vet es KAWS-t'n?

287. That is too much.

דאָס איז צו פֿיל.

DAWS iz TSOO FEEL.

288. Please drive more slowly (carefully).

זײַט אַזױ גוט, פֿאָרט פּאַמעלעכער (אָפּגעהיטער).

*ZIT ah-zoy GOOT, FORT pah-MEH-leh-khehr
(AWP-geh-hee-ter).*

289. Stop here.

שטעלט זיך דאָ אָפּ.

SHTELT zikh DAW AWP.

290. Wait for me.

װאַרט אױף מיר.

VAHRT oyf meer.

AUTOMOBILE

291. How do I obtain a driver's license?

װי קריג איך אַ פֿירליצענץ?

VEE KRIG eekh ah FEER-lee-tsents?

292. When does it open (close)?

ווען עפֿנט (פֿאַרמאַכט) ער זיך?

VEN EH-f'nt (fahr-MAHKHT) ehr zikh?

293. Where is a gas station (a garage)?

וואו איז פֿאַראַן אַ גאַזאָלין־סטאַנציע (אַ גאַראַזש)?

*VOO iz fah-RAHN ah gah-zaw-LEEN-stahnts-yeh
(ah gah-RAHZH)?*

294. Is the road good (paved)?

צי איז דער וועג אַ גוטער (אַ ברוקירטער)?

tsee iz dehr VEG ah GOO-tehr (ah broo-KEER-tehr)?

295. What town is this (the next one)?

וואָסער שטעטל איז דאָס (דאָס קומענדיקע)?

*VAW-sehr SHTEH-t'l iz DAWS (daws KOO-men-
dee-keh)?*

296. Where does that road go?

וואוהין פֿירט יענער וועג?

voo-HEEN FEERT YEH-nehr VEG?

297. Can you show it to me on the map?

צי קענט איר מיר עס ווײַזן אויף דער קאַרטע?

tsee KENT eer meer es VI-z'n oyf dehr KAR-teh?

298. The automobile club.

דער אויטאָקלוב.

dehr OY-taw-kloob.

299. I have a driver's license.

איך האָב אַ פֿירליצענץ.

eekh HAWB ah FEER-lee-tsents.

300. How much is gas a gallon?

וויפֿל קאָסט אַ גאַלאָן גאַזאָלין?

VEE-f'l COST ah gah-LAWN gah-zaw-LEEN?

301. Give me —— gallons.

גיט מיר —— גאַלאָן.

GIT meer —— gah-LAWN.

302. Please change the oil.

זײַט אַזױ גוט, בײַט. אױס די אײל.

ZIT ah-zoy GOOT, BIT OYS dee AYL.

303. Light (medium, heavy) oil.

לײַכטע (מיטעלע, שװערע) אײל.

LIKH-teh (MIT-eh-leh, SHVEH-reh) AYL.

304. Put water in the battery.

גיסט צו װאַסער אין דער באַטעריע.

GEEST TSOO VAH-sehr in dehr bah-TEHR-yeh.

305. Recharge it.

לאָדט זי אָן צוריק.

LAWT zee AWN tsoo-RIK.

306. Will you lubricate the car?

צי װעט איר אָנשמירן דעם אױטאָ?

tsee vet eer AWN-shmee-r'n dem OY-taw?

307. Could you wash it now (soon)?

צי קענט איר אים איצט (באַלד) אָפּװאַשן?

tsee KENT eer im ITST (BAHLD) AWP-vah-sh'n?

308. Tighten the brakes.

פֿאַרשטײפֿט דעם טאָרמאָז.

fahr-SHTIFT dem TAWR-mawz.

309. Will you check the tires?

צי קענט איר קאָנטראָלירן די רײפֿן?

tsee KENT eer kawnt-raw-LEE-r'n dee RAY-f'n?

310. Can you fix the flat tire?

צי קענט איר פֿאַרריכטן דעם געפּלאַצטן רײף?

tsee KENT eer fahr-REEKH-t'n dem geh-PLAHTS-t'n RAYF?

311. Can you recommend a good mechanic?

צי קענט איר רעקאָמענדירן אַ גוטן מעכאַניקער?

tsee KENT eer reh-kaw-men-DEE-r'n ah GOO-t'n meh-KHAH-nee-kehr?

312. I want some air.

איך דאַרף לופֿט.

eekh DAHRF LOOFT.

313. A puncture.

אַ לאָך.

ah LAWKH.

314. The —— does not work well.

דער —— פֿונקציאָנירט ניט גוט.

dehr —— foonkts-yaw-NEERT nit GOOT.

315. What is wrong?

וואָס איז דער מער?

VAWS iz dehr MEHR?

316. There is a grinding (a leak, a noise).

עס רייבט זיך (עס רינט, עס קלאַפּט).

es RIPT zikh (es RINT, es KLAHPT).

317. The engine overheats.

דער מאָטאָר הייצט זיך אָן צו שטאַרק.

dehr maw-TAWR HITST zikh AWN TSOO SHTAHRK.

318. The engine misses (stalls).

דער מאָטאָר לאָזט דורך אַן אויפֿריס (פֿאַר־האַקט זיך).

dehr maw-TAWR lawst DOQRKH ahn OYF-rîs (far-HAHKT zikh).

319. **May I park here for a while?**

צי קען איך דאָ אַ ווײלע פּאַרקן?

tsee KEN eekh daw ah VI-leh PAHR-k'n?

320. **I want to garage my car for the night.**

איך וויל לאָזן מײַן אויטאָ אין אַ גאַראַזש אויף
דער נאַכט.

*eekh VIL LAW-z'n mīn OY-taw in ah gah-RAHZH
oyf dehr NAHKHT.*

321. **The traffic light.**

דער פֿאַרקערלאָמפּ.

dehr fahr-KEHR-lawmp.

322. **The traffic court.**

דאָס פֿאַרקער-געריכט.

daws fahr-KEHR-geh-reekht.

323. **The summons.**

דער רופֿצעטל.

dehr ROOF-tseh-t'l.

HELP ON THE ROAD

324. **I am sorry to trouble you.**

זײַט מוחל וואָס איך בין איך מאַטריח.

zīt MOY-kh'l vaws eekh bin īkh maht-REE-ahkh.

325. **My car has broken down.**

מײַן אויטאָ איז קאַליע געוואָרן.

mīn OY-taw iz KAHL-yeh geh-VAW-r'n.

326. **Can you tow (push) me?**

צי קענט איר מיך צושלעפּן (אַ שטופּ טאָן)?

*tsee KENT eer mikh TSOO-shleh-p'n (ah SHTOOP
tawn)?*

327. Can you give me a lift to ——?

צי קענט איר מיך אונטערפֿירן ביז ——?

tsee KENT eer mikh OON-tehr-fee-r'n biz ——?

328. Can you help me jack up the car?

צי קענט איר מיר העלפֿן אונטערהייבן דעם
אויטאָ?

*tsee KENT eer meer HEL-f'n OON-tehr-hay-b'n dem
OY-taw?*

329. Will you help me put on the spare?

צי ווילט איר מיר העלפֿן אָנטאָן די זאַפּאַסרייף?

*tsee VILT eer meer HEL-f'n AWN-tawn dee zah-
PAHS-rayf?*

330. Could you give me some gas?

צי קענט איר מיר געבן אַ ביסל גאַזאָלין?

*tsee KENT eer meer GEH-b'n ah BISS'l gah-zaw-
LEEN?*

331. Can you take me to a garage?

צי קענט איר מיך צופֿירן ביז אַ גאַראָשש?

*tsee KENT eer mikh TSOO-fee-r'n biz ah gah-
RAHZH?*

332. Can you help me get the car off the road?

צי קענט איר מיר העלפֿן אַראָפּפֿירן דעם
אויטאָ פֿון וועג?

*tsee KENT eer meer HEL-f'n ah-RAWP-fee-r'n dem
OY-taw foon VEG?*

333. My car is stuck in the mud.

מײַן אויטאָ איז געבליבן שטעקן אין בלאָטע.

mîn OY-taw iz geh-BLIB'n SH'TEH-k'n in BLAW-teh.

334. It is in the ditch.

ער איז אין גראָבן.

eht iz in GRAW-b'n.

PARTS OF THE CAR

335. The accelerator.
דער אַקצעלעראָטאָר•
dehr ahk-tseh-leh-RAH-tawr.

336. The battery.
די באַטעריע•
dee bah-TEHR-yeh.

337. The bolt.
דער שרויף•
dehr SHROYF.

338. The brake.
דער טאָרמאָז•
dehr TAWR-mawz.

339. The headlight.
דער פֿאָנאָר•
dehr faw-NAR.

340. The horn.
דער טרומייט•
dehr troo-MAYT.

341. The nut.
די מוטער•
dee MOO-tehr.

342. The spring.
די ספּרונזשינע•
dee sproon-ZHIN-eh.

343. The starter.
דער סטאַרטער•
dehr STAHR-tehr.

344. The steering wheel.
דער קערעווער•
dehr KEH-reh-vehr.

345. The tail light.
דאָס הינטערשטע לעמפּל•
daws HEEN-tehrsh-teh LEM-p'l.

346. The tire.
די רייף.
dee RAYF.

347. The spare tire.
די זאפאסרייף.
dee zah-PAHS-rayf.

348. The wheel.
די ראָד.
dee RAWD.

349. The windshield wiper.
דער פֿענצטער־וױשער.
dehr FENTS-tehr-vee-shehr.

TOOLS AND EQUIPMENT

350. The chains.
די קייטן.
dee KAY-t'n.

351. The hammer.
דער האַמער.
dehr HAH-mehr.

352. The jack.
דער אונטערהייבער.
dehr OON-tehr-hay-behr.

353. The key.
דער שליסל.
dehr SHLEE-s'l.

354. The pliers.
די צוואַנג.
dee TSVAHNGG.

355. The rope.
דער שטריק.
dehr SHTRIK.

356. The screwdriver.
דער שרויפֿן־ציער.
dehr SHROY-f'n-tsee-ehr.

357. The tire pump.

די רייפֿפּאָמפּע•

dee RAYF-pawm-peh.

358. The wrench.

דער מוטער־דרייער•

dehr MOO-tehr-dray-ehr.

HOTEL AND APARTMENT

359. Which hotel (boarding house, rooming house) is good (inexpensive)?

וועלכער האָטעל (פּאַנסיאָן· הויז מיט מעבלירטע
צימערן) איז גוט (ביליק)

VEL-khehr haw-TEL (pahns-YAWN, HOYZ mit meb-LEER-teh TSIM-eh-r'n) iz GOOT (BIL-ik)?

360. The best hotel.

דער בעסטער האָטעל•

dehr BES-tehr haw-TEL.

361. Not too expensive.

ניט צו טײַער•

NIT TSOO TI-ehr.

362. I (do not) want to be in the center of town.

איך וויל (ניט) זײַן אין צענטער שטאָט•

eekh VIL (nit) ZIN in TSEN-tehr SHTAWT.

363. Where it is not noisy.

וואָ עס איז ניט טומלדיק•

voo es iz NIT TOO-m'l-dik.

364. I have a reservation for ——.

איך האָב אַ רעזערוואַציע אויף ——•

eekh HAWB ah reh-zehr-VAHTS-yeh oyf ——.

365. I want to reserve a room.

איך וויל רעזערווירן אַ צימער•

eekh VIL reh-zehr-VEE-r'n ah TSIM-ehr.

366. I want a room with (without) meals.

איך װיל אַ צימער מיט (אָן) מאָלצײטן•

eekh VIL ah TSIM-ehr MIT (AWN) MAWL-tsī-
t'n.

367. A room with a double bed.

אַ צימער מיט אַ טאָפּלבעט•

ah TSIM-ehr mit ah TAW-p'l-bet.

368. A single bed.

די אײנציקע בעט•

dee AYN-tsik-eh BET.

369. Twin beds.

די צװילינגבעט•

dee TSVEE-lingg-bet.

370. A suite.

אַ סװיטע•

ah SVEE-teh.

371. With a bath (a shower).

מיט אַ װאַנע (אַ שפּריץ)•

mit ah VAH-neh (ah SHPRITS).

372. With a window (a porch).

מיט אַ פֿענצטער (אַ גאַניק)•

mit ah FENTS-tehr (ah GAH-nik).

373. For —— days.

אויף —— טעג•

oyf —— TEG.

374. For tonight.

אויף הינט•

oyf HINT.

375. For —— persons.

פֿאַר —— מענטשן•

fahr —— MEN-ch'n.

376. What is the rate per day?

װיפֿל קאָסט אַ טאָג•

VEE-f'l COST ah TAWG?

377. A week.

אַ װאָך•

ah VAWKH.

378. A month.

אַ חודש•

ah KHOY-desh.

379. On what floor?
אויף דעם וויפֿלטן גאָרן?
oyf dem VEE-f'l-t'n GAW-r'n?

380. Stairs.   **381. Upstairs.**   **382. Downstairs**
טרעפּ·   אויבן·   אונטן·
TREP.   *OY-b'n.*   *OON-t'n.*

383. Is there an elevator?
צי איז פֿאַראַן אַ ליפֿט?
tsee iz fah-RAHN ah LIFT?

384. Running water.   **385. Hot water.**
פֿליסנדיק וואַסער·   הייס וואַסער·
FLEE-s'n-dik VAH-sehr.   *HAYS VAH-sehr.*

386. I want a front (back) room.
איך וויל אַ פֿאָדערשטן (הינטערשטן) צימער·
eekh VIL ah FAW-dehrsh-t'n (HIN-tehrsh-t'n) TSIM-ehr.

387. On a lower floor.   **388. Higher up.**
אויף אַ נידעריקערן גאָרן·   העכער·
oyf ah NID-eh-ree-keh-r'n GAW-r'n.   *HEH-khehr.*

389. I should like to see the room.
איך וואָלט וועלן זען דעם צימער·
eekh vawlt VEH-l'n ZEN dem TSIM-ehr.

390. I (I do not) like this room.
דער צימער געפֿעלט מיר (ניט)·
dehr TSIM-ehr geh-FELT meer (nit).

391. With more light.   **392. More air.**
מיט מער ליכט·   מער לופֿט·
mit MEHR LEEKHT.   *MEHR LOOFT.*

393. Please sign the hotel register.

זיט אזױ גוט, פֿאַרשריבט זיך אין האָטעל־
פּינקס·

*ZIT ah-zoy GOOT, fahr-SHRIPT zikh in haw-
TEL-pin-kes.*

394. I have baggage at the station.

איך האָב באַגאַזש אױף דער סטאַנציע·

eekh hawb bah-GAHZH oyf dehr STAHNTS-yeh.

395. Will you send for my bags?

צי קענט איר שיקן נאָך מינע טשעמאָדאַנעס?

*tsee KENT eer SHIK'n nawkh MI-neh cheh-maw-
DAW-nes?*

396. Here is the check for my trunk.

אָט איז די קװיטונג פֿאַר מין קאָפֿער·

AWT eez dee KVIT-oongg fahr min KAW-fehr.

397. Please send bath towels to my room.

זיט אזױ גוט, שיקט אַרױף באַדהאַנטעכער אין
מין צימער·

*ZIT ah-zoy GOOT, SHIKT ah-ROYF BAWD-
hahn-teh-khehr in min TSIM-ehr.*

398. Washcloths.

די װאַשטיכלעך·

*dee VAHSH-teekh-
lekh.*

399. Face towels.

די האַנטעכער צום פֿנים·

*dee HAHN-teh-khehr
tsoom PAW-nim.*

400. Ice.

דאָס אײַז·

daws IZ.

401. Ice water.

דאָס אײַזװאַסער·

daws IZ-vah-sehr.

402. A messenger.

אַ שיקײַנגל·

ah SHIK-yin-g'l.

403. Room service.

באַדינונג אין צימער·

*bah-DEE-noongg in
TSIM-ehr.*

404. How much should I tip the maid?

ווי‏פֿל טרינקגעלט זאָל איך געבן דער אויפֿרא־
מעריז?

VEE-f'l TRINK-gelt zawl eekh GEH-b'n dehr OYF-
rah-meh-r'n?

405. Please call me at —— o'clock.

זײַט·אַזוי גוט‏, רופֿט מיך —— אַ זײגער·

ZIT ah-zoy GOOT, ROOFT mikh —— ah ZAY-
gehr.

406. I want breakfast in my room.

איך וויל פֿרישטיק אין מײן צימער·

eekh VIL FRISH-tik in min TSIM-ehr.

407. Could I have some laundry done?

צי קען איך לאָזן אויסוואַשן אַ ביסל וועש?

tsee KEN eekh LAW-z'n OYS-vah-sh'n ah BISS'l
VESH?

408. I want some things pressed.

איך וויל לאָזן אויספּרעסן עטלעכע זאַכן·

eekh vil LAW-z'n OYS-preh-s'n ET-leh-kheh ZAH-
kh'n.

409. I should like to speak to the manager.

איך וואָלט וועלן רעדן מיט דעם פֿאַרוואַלטער·

eekh vawlt VEH-l'n REH-d'n mit dem fahr-VAHL-
tehr.

410. My room key, please.

מײן צימער־שליסל‏, זײַט אַזוי גוט·

min TSIM-ehr-shlee-s'l, ZIT ah-zoy GOOT.

411. Have I any letters?

צי זײַנען פֿאַראַן פֿאַר מיר בריוו?

tsee zi-nen fah-RAHN fahr meer PREEV?

412. Where do you live?

וואו וואוינט איר?

VOO VOYNT eer?

413. I want a furnished room with use of the kitchen.

איך וויל אַ מעבלירט צימער מיט קיכבאַנוץ.

eekh VIL ah meb-LEERT TSIM-ehr mit KEEKH-bah-noots.

414. Must we pay in advancce?

צי מוזן מיר צאָלן אין פֿאָרויס?

tsee MOO-z'n meer TSAW-l'n in faw-ROYS?

415. When can I move in?

ווען קען איך זיך אַריינקליבן?

VEN ken eekh zikh ah-RIN-klĭ-b'n?

416. May I have the keys?

צי קען איך האָבן די שליסלען?

tsee KEN eekh HAW-b'n dee SHLIS-len?

417. Rooms to let.

צימערן צו פֿאַרדינגען.

TSIM-eh-r'n tsoo fahr-DIN-gen.

418. We have no rooms (apartments) for rent.

מיר האָבן ניט קיין צימערן (דירות) צו פֿאַר־
דינגען.

meer HAW-b'n nit kayn TSIM-eh-r'n (DEE-res) tsoo fahr-DIN-gen.

419. The rent is payable in advance.

דאָס דירה־געלט מוז מען צאָלן אין פֿאָרויס.

daws DEE-reh-gehlt MOOZ men TSAW-l'n in faw-ROYS.

420. I live on the second (on the top) floor.

איך װוין אױפֿן צװײטן (אױפֿן אײבערשטן) גאָרן·

eekh VOYN oy-f'n TSVAY-t'n (oy-f'n AY-behrsh-t'n)
GAW-r'n.

421. I want to rent a place for the summer.

איך װיל דינגען אַן אָרט אױפֿן זומער·

eekh vil DIN-gen ahn ORT oy-f'n ZOO-mehr.

422. Is there a private bath?

צי איז פֿאַראַן אַ פּריװאַטע װאַנע?

tsee iz fah-RAHN ah pree-VAH-teh VAH-neh?

423. Are the beds comfortable?

צי זײַנען די בעטן באַקװעמע?

tsee zī-nen dee BEH-t'n bahk-VEH-meh?

424. Is the linen furnished?

צי װערט פֿאַרזאָרגט בעטגעװאַנט און האַנטע־
כער?

tsee vehrt fahr-ZORKT BET-geh-vahnt oon HAHN-
teh-khehr?

425. How much is it a month?

װיפֿל קאָסט אַ חודש?

VEE-f'l COST ah KHOY-desh?

426. Do you know a good cook (a maid)?

צי קענט איר אַ גוטע קעכין (אַ דינסט)?

tsee KENTeer ah GOO-teh KEH-kh'n(ah DEENST)?

427. Where can I rent a garage?

צי קען איך דינגען אַ גאַראַזש?

tsee KEN eekh DIN-gen ah gah-RAHZH?

428. How much do I owe you?

װיפֿל קומט איך?

VEE-f'l KOOMT ĭkh?

THE HOME: USEFUL WORDS

429. The apartment.
די דירה.
dee DEF-reh.

430. The bathroom.
דער וואַנע־צימער.
dehr VAH-neh-tsee-mehr.

431. The bed (single, double).
די בעט (אײנציקע, טאָפּל־).
dee BET (AYN-tsi-keh, TAW-p'l-).

432. The bedroom.   **433. The bell.**
דער שלאָפֿצימער.   דאָס גלעקל.
dehr SHLAWF-tsee-mehr.   *daws GLEH-k'l.*

434. The blanket.
די קאָלדרע.
dee KAWLD-reh.

435. The bureau.
דער קאָמאָד.
dehr kaw-MAWD.

436. The carpet.
דער טעפּעך.
dehr TEH-pekh.

437. The ceiling.
די סטעליע.
dee STEL-yeh.

438. The cellar.
דער קעלער.
dehr KEH-lehr.

439. The chair.
די שטול.
dee SHTOOL.

440. The coffee pot.
דער קאװעניק.
dehr KAH-veh-nik.

441. The cook.
די קעכין.
dee KEH-kh'n.

442. The curtains.
דער פֿאָרהאַנג.
dehr FAWR-hahngg.

443. The dining room.
דער עסצימער.
dehr ES-tsee-mehr.

444. The dishes.
די כלים.
dee KAY-lim.

445. The door.
די טיר.
dee TEER.

446. The electric bulb.
דאָס עלעקטרישע לעמפּל.
daws eh-LEK-trih-sheh LEM-p'l.

447. The fan.
דער װענטילאַטאָר.
dehr ven-tee-LAH-tor.

448. The flat.
די דירה.
dee DEE-reh.

449. The floor.
די פּאָדלאָגע.
dec pahd-LAW-geh.

450. The furniture.
די מעבל־
dee MEH-b'l.

451. The garden.
דער גאָרטן־
dehr GOR-t'n.

452. The gas meter.
דער גאַזמעטער־
dehr GAHZ-mes-tehr.

453. The gas range.
די גאַזפּליטע־
dee GAHZ-plee-teh.

454. The hall.
דער קאָרידאָר־
dehr kaw-ree-DAWR.

455. The iron.
דאָס פּרעסל־
daws PREH-s'l.

456. The ironing board.
די פּרעסברעט־
dee PRES-bret.

457. The key.
דער שליסל־
dehr SHLEE-s'l.

458. The kitchen.
די קיך־
dee KEEKH.

459. The lamp.
דער לאָמפּ־
dehr LAWMP.

460. The lavatory.
דער קלאָזעט·
dehr klaw-ZET.

461. The linen.
דאָס וועש·
daws VESH.

462. The living room.
דער וואוינצימער·
dehr VOYN-tsee-mehr.

463. The mattress.
דער מאַטראַץ·
dehr maht-RAHTS.

464. The mirror.
דער שפיגל·
dehr SHPEE-g'l.

465. The nursery.
דער קינדער־צימער·
dehr KIN-dehr-tsee-mehr.

466. The oven.
דער אויוון·
dehr OY-v'n.

467. The pan.
די סקאָווראָדע·
dee SKAWV-raw-deh.

468. The pantry.
די שפּיזקאַמער·
dee SHPIZ-kah-mehr.

469. The pillow.
דער קישן·
dehr KEE-sh'n.

470. The quilt.
די פּערענע׃
dee PEH-reh-neh.

471. The refrigerator.
דער פֿרידזשידער׃
dehr free-jee-DEHR.

472. The rent.
דאָס דירה־געלט׃
daws DEE-reh-gelt.

473. The roof.
דער דאַך׃
dehr DAHKH.

474. The room.
דער צימער׃
dehr TSIM-ehr.

475. The saucepan.
דאָס פֿענדל׃
daws FEN-d'l.

476. The silverware.
די גאָפּל־לעפֿל׃
dee gaw-p'l-LEH-f'l.

477. The tea kettle.
דער טשײַניק׃
dehr CHĪ-nik.

478. The wall.
די וואַנט׃
dee VAHNT.

479. The window.
דער פֿענצטער׃
dehr FENTS-tehr.

CAFÉ

480. The bartender.

דער באַרמאַן.

dehr BAR-mahn.

481. A cocktail.

אַ קאָקטייל.

ah COCK-tail.

482. A drink.

אַ געטראַנק.

ah geh-TRANK.

483. A liqueur.

אַ ליקער.

ah lee-KEHR.

484. A fruit drink.

אַ פֿרוכטגעטראַנק.

ah FROOKHT-geh-trahnk.

485. A non-alcoholic drink.

אַ ניט־אַלקאָהאָלישער געטראַנק.

ah NIT-ahl-kaw-HAW-lee-shehr geh-TRAHNK.

486. A small (large) bottle of ——.

אַ פֿלעשל (פֿלאַש) ——.

ah FLEH-sh'l (FLAHSH) ——.

487. A glass of ——.

אַ גלאָז ——.

ah GLAWZ ——.

488. Beer (light, dark).

ביר (העלע, טונקעלע).

BEER (HEH-leh, TOON-keh-leh).

489. Wine (red, white).

וויַן (רויטער, וויַסער).

VIN (ROY-tehr, VI-sehr).

490. Whiskey (and soda).

וויסקי (מיט סאָדע).

VIS-kee (mit SAW-deh).

491. Cognac.
קאָניאַק׃
KAWN-yahk.

492. Champagne.
שאַמפּאַניער׃
shahm-PAHN-yehr.

493. To your health.
לחיים׃
leh-KHAH-yim.

494. Let's have another.
לאָמיר נאָך אַ מאָל אויסטרינקען
LAW-meer NAWKH ah mawl OYS-trin-ken.

RESTAURANT

495. Where is there a good restaurant?
וואו איז דאָ אַ גוטער רעסטאָראַן?
VOO iz daw ah GOO-tehr res-taw-RAHN?

496. A dairy restaurant.
אַ מילכיקער רעסטאָראַן׃
ah MIL-khee-kehr res-taw-RAHN.

497. A kosher restaurant.
אַ כשרער רעסטאָראַן׃
ah KAW-sheh-rehr res-taw-RAHN.

498. Breakfast.
פרישטיק׃
FRISH-tik.

499. Lunch.
לאָנטש׃
lunch.

500. Dinner.
מיטאָג׃
MIT-awg.

501. Supper.
וועטשערע׃
VEH-cheh-reh.

502. A sandwich.
אַ סענדוויטש׃
ah SEND-vich.

503. Snack.
איבערבײַסן׃
EE-behr-bĭ-s'n.

504. At what time is dinner served?

װיפֿל אַ זײגער דערלאַנגט מען מיטאָג?

VEE-f'l ah ZAY-gehr dehr-LAHNKT men MIT-awg?

505. The waitress.

די קעלנערין.

dee KEL-neh-r'n.

506. The waiter.

דער קעלנער.

dehr KEL-nehr.

507. The headwaiter.

דער הויפּטקעלנער.

dehr HOYPT-kel-nehr.

508. Waiter!

קעלנער!

KEL-nehr!

509. There are two (five) of us.

מיר זײנען זאַלבעצװײט (זאַלבעפֿינפֿט).

meer zī-nen zahl-beh-TSVAYT (zahl-beh-FINFT).

510. Give me a table inside (outside, near the window).

גיט מיר אַ טיש אינעװייניק (אין דרויסן, בײם פֿענצטער).

GEET meer ah TISH IN-vay-nik (in DROY-s'n, bīm FENTS-tehr).

511. At the side.

בײ דער זײט.

bī dehr ZIT.

512. In the corner.

אין װינקל.

in VIN-k'l.

513. Is this table reserved?

צי איז דער טיש רעזערװירט?

tsee iz DEHR TISH reh-zehr-VEERT?

514. That one will be free soon.

יענער װעט באַלד זײן פֿרײ.

YEH-nehr vet bahld zīn FRI.

515. Where can I wash up?

װאו קען איך זיך אַרומװאַשן?

VOO ken eekh zikh ah-ROOM-vah-sh'n?

516. Please serve us quickly.

זיט אַזױ גוט, באַדינט אונדז גיך.

ZIT ah-zoy GOOT, bah-DEENT oondz GEEKH.

517. We want to dine à la carte.

מיר װילן עסן אַ לאַ קאַרט.

meer VIL'n EH-s'n ah lah KART.

518. What is the specialty of the house?

װאָס איז די ספּעציאַליטעט פֿון רעסטאָראַן?

VAWS eez dee spehts-yah-lee-TET foon res-taw-RAHN?

519. Bring me the menu (the wine list).

ברענגט מיר דעם מעניו (די װײַנליסטע).

BRENGT meer dem meh-NEW (dee VIN-lis-teh).

520. A plate.

אַ טעלער.

ah TEH-lehr.

521. A knife.

אַ מעסער.

ah MEH-sehr.

522. A fork.

אַ גאָפּל.

ah GAW-p'l.

523. A large spoon.

אַ גרױסער לעפֿל.

ah GROY-sehr LEH-f'l.

524. A teaspoon.

אַ לעפֿעלע.

ah LEH-feh-leh.

525. This is not clean.

דאָס איז ניט רײן.

daws eez NIT RAYN.

526. (A little) more of this.

נאָך (אַ ביסל) פֿון דעם.

NAWKH (ah bis'l) foon DEM.

527. I have had enough, thanks.

דאָס איז גענוג, אַ דאַנק.

DAWS iz geh-NOOG, ah DAHNK.

528. I want something simple.

איך וויל עפעס פשוטס.

eekh VIL eh-pes PAW-shets.

529. Not too spicy.

ניט צו בשמימדיק.

NIT TSOO BSAW-mim-dik.

530. I like the meat cooked rare (well done).

איך האָב האָלט אַז דאָס פלייש איז ניט דער־
בראָטן (גוט דורכגעבראָטן).

*eekh hawb HAWLT ahz daws FLAYSH eez NIT
dehr-BRAW-t'n (GOOT DOORKH-geh-braw-t'n).*

531. This is overcooked.

דאָס איז איבערגעקאָכט.

daws iz EE-behr-geh-kawkht.

532. This is undercooked.

דאָס איז ניט דערקאָכט.

daws iz NIT dehr-KAWKHT.

533. This is too tough (sweet, sour).

דאָס איז צו האַרט (זיס, זויער).

daw iz TSOO HART (ZEES, ZOY-ehr).

534. This is cold.

דאָס איז קאַלט.

daws iz KAHLT.

535. Take it away, please.

נעמט עס צו, זיט אַזוי גוט.

NEMT es TSOO, ZIT ah-zoy GOOT.

536. I did not order this.

איך האָב דאָס ניט באַשטעלט.

eekh hawb daws NIT bah-SHTELT.

537. May I change this for ——?

צי קען איך דאָס אויסבײַטן אויף ——?

tsee KEN eekh daws OYS-bĭ-t'n oyf ——?

538. May I see your pastries?

צי קען איך זען אײַערע געבעקסן?

tsee KEN eekh ZEN ah-yeh-reh geh-BEK-s'n?

539. Ask the head waiter to come here.

בעט דעם הויפטקעלנער קומען אַהער•

BET dem HOYPT-kel-nehr KOO-men ah-HEHR.

540. The check, please.

דעם חשבון, זײַט אַזױ גוט•

dem KHESH-b'n, ZĬT ah-zoy GOOT.

541. Is the tip included?

צי איז דאָס טרינקגעלט אײַנגערעכנט?

tsee iz daws TRINK-gelt ah-RĬN-geh-reh-kh'nt?

542. Is the service charge included?

צי איז דער באַדינונג-אָפּצאָל אײַנגערעכנט?

tsee iz dehr bah-DEE-noongg-awp-tsawl ah-RĬN-geh-reh-kh'nt?

543. What are these charges for?

פֿאַר װאָס האָט איר דאָ גערעכנט?

fahr VAWS hawt eer daw geh-REH-kh'nt?

544. There is a mistake in the bill.

עס איז פֿאַראַן אַ טעות אין חשבון•

es iz fah-RAHN ah TAW-es in KHESH-b'n.

545. Keep the change.

האַלט דעם רעשט פֿאַר זיך•

HAHLT dem RESHT fahr ZEEKH.

546. Kindly pay at the cashier's.

זײַט אַזױ גוט, באַצאָלט בײַ דער קאַסע•

ZĬT ah-zoy GOOT, bah-TSAWLT bĭ dehr KAH-seh.

FOOD:
BREADS AND BREAKFAST FOODS

547. The bread.

דאָס ברויט.

daws BROYT.

548. Bagels.

בייגל.

BAY-g'l.

549. Butter (salted, sweet).

פּוטער (געזאַלצענע, זיסע).

POO-tehr (geh-ZAHL-tseh-neh, ZEE-seh).

550. Cereal (cooked, dry).

קאַשע (געקאָכטע, טרוקענע).

KAH-sheh (geh-KAWKH-teh, TROO-keh-neh).

551. Cream cheese.

קרעמקעז.

KREM-kez.

552. Eggs (fried, hard boiled, soft boiled, poached).

אייער (געפּרעגלטע, האַרטע, ווייכע, געקאָכטע אָן שאַלעכץ).

AY-ehr (geh-PREH-g'l-teh, HAHR-teh, VAY-kheh, geh-KAWKH-teh AWN SHAW-lekhts).

553. Scrambled eggs.

פֿינקוקן.

FIN-koo-kh'n.

554. Hallah.

חלה.

KHAH-leh.

555. Juice (orange, prune, tomato).

זאַפֿט (פֿון מאַראַנצן, פֿלוימען, טאָמאַטן).

ZAHFT (foon mah-RAHN-ts'n, FLOY-men, taw-MAH-t'n).

556. Lox.
לאַקס.
lahx.

557. Matzo.
מצה.
MAH-tseh.

558. Matzo brei.
מצה־ברײ.
MAH-tseh-brī.

559. Onion rolls.
ציבעלע־בולקעס.
TSIB-eh-leh-bool-kes.

560. Pumpernickel.
פּאָמפּערניקל.
pawm-pehr-NIK'l.

561. Rolls.
בולקעס.
BOOL-kes.

562. Rye bread (with seeds).
קאָרנברױט (מיט קימל).
KAW-r'n-broyt (mit KIM'l).

563. Toast and jelly (jam).
טאָסט מיט אײַנגעמאַכטס (פּאַווידלע).
TOAST mit ÍN-geh-mahkhts (PAW-vid-leh).

APPETIZERS
564. Filled fish.
געפֿילטע פֿיש.
geh-FIL-teh FISH.

565. Smoked fish (lox).
גערייכערטע פֿיש (לאַקס)·
geh-RAY-khehr-teh FISH (LAHX).

566. Grapefruit.
גרייפּפֿרוט·
GRAYP-froot.

567. Chopped herring.
געהאַקטע הערינג·
geh-HAHK-teh HEH-ringg.

568. Pickled herring.
מאַרינירטע הערינג·
mah-ree-NEER-teh HEH-ringg.

569. Chopped liver.
געהאַקטע לעבער·
geh-HAHK-teh LEH-behr.

570. Melon.
מעלאָן·
meh-LAWN.

571. Pickles.
זויערע אוגערקעס·
ZOY-eh-reh OO-gehr-kes.

572. (Greek) Salad.
(גריכישער) סאַלאַד·
(GREE-khee-shehr)sah-LAHT.

573. Sardines.
סאַרדינקעס·
sahr-DIN-kes.

574. Sauerkraut.
זויערע קרויט·
ZOY-eh-reh KROYT.

SOUPS

575. Borscht.
בארשט·
borsht.

576. Barley soup.
פערל־גרויפן ־זוף·
PEH-r'l-groy-p'n-zoop.

577. Chicken broth (with noodles).
יויך (מיט לאָקשן)·
YOYKH (mit LAWK-sh'n).

578. Matzo balls.
קנײדלעך·
KNAYD-lekh.

579. Schav.
שטשאוו·
shchahv.

580. Split pea soup.
ארבעסזופ·
AHR-bes-zoop.

581. Potato.
קאַרטאָפל·
kahr-TAW-f'l.

582. Vegetable.
גרינסן·
GREEN-s'n.

VEGETABLES

583. Beans.
פאַסאָליעס·
fah-SAWL-yes.

584. Beets.
בוריקעס·
BOO-ree-kes.

585. Carrots.
מערן·
MEH-r'n.

586. Cauliflower.
קאַליפיאַרן·
kah-leef-YAW-r'n.

587. Celery.
סעלעריע·
seh-LEHR-yeh.

588. Cucumbers.
אוגערקעס·
OO-gehr-kes.

589. Lettuce.
סאַלאַט·
sah-LAHT.

590. Mushrooms.
שוועמלעך·
SHVEM-lekh.

591. Onions.
ציבעלעס·
TSIB-eh-les.

592. Peas.
אַרבעס·
AHR-bes.

593. Peppers.
פעפער·
FEH-fehr.

594. Potatoes (boiled, baked, fried).

קאַרטאָפֿל (געקאָכטע, געבאַקענע, געפֿרעגל־
טע)·

*kahr-TAW-f'l (geh-KAWKH-teh, geh-BAH-keh-neh,
geh-PREH-g'l-teh).*

595. Radishes.

רעטעכלעך·

REH-tekh-lekh.

596. Spinach.

שפּינאַט·

shpee-NAHT.

597. Tomatos.

טאָמאַטן·

taw-MAH-t'n.

598. Tsimmis.

צימעס·

TSIM-es.

ENTRÉES

599. Beef (boiled, roast).

רינדערנס (געקאָכט, געבראָטן)·

RIN-deh-r'ns (gah-KAWKHT, geh-BRAW-t'n).

600. Corned beef.

פֿעקלפֿלייש·

PEH-k'l-flaysh.

601. Blintzes.

בלינצעס·

BLIN-tses

602. Bologna.

באַלאָניער וואָרשט·

baw-LAWN-yehr VOORSHT.

603. Stuffed cabbage.
האלובצעס׃
HAW-loob-tses.

604. Capon (roast).
קאפהאן (געבראטענער)׃
KAHP-hawn (geh-BRAW-teh-nehr).

605. Carp.
קארפ׃
kahrp.

606. Chicken (boiled, roasted).
הון (געקאכט׳ געבראטן)׃
HOON (geh-KAWKHT, geh-BRAW-t'n).

607. Chicken fricassee.
געהאקטע הון׃
geh-HAHK-teh HOON.

608. Cold cuts.
אויפשניט׃
OYF-shnit.

609. Stuffed derma.
געפילטע קישקע׃
geh-FIL-teh KISH-keh.

610. Duck.
קאטשקע׃
KAHCH-keh.

611. Eggs with salami (bologna).
אייער מיט סאלאמי (באלאניער ווארשט)׃
*AY-ehr mit sah-LAH-mee (baw-LAWN-yehr
VOORSHT).*

612. Fish (fried, baked, boiled).
פיש (געפרעגלטע געבאקענע׳ געקאכטע)׃
*FISH (geh-PREH-g'l-teh, geh-BAH-keh-neh, geh-
KAWKH-teh).*

613. Frankfurters and baked beans.

װאָרשטלעך מיט געבאַקענע בעבלעך׃

VOORSHT-lekh mit geh-BAH-keh-neh BEB-lekh.

614. Goose.

גאַנדז׃

gahndz.

615. Goulash.

גולאַש׃

GOO-lahsh.

616. Knishes.

קנישעס

K'NISH-es.

617. Kreplach.

קרעפּלעך׃

KREP-lekh.

618. Kugel (matzo, potato).

קוגל (פֿון מצה, קאַרטאָפֿל)׃

KOO-g'l (foon MAH-tseh, kahr-TAW-f'l).

619. Lamb (chops, stew).

שעפּסנפֿלײש (קאָטלעטן, גולאַש)׃

SHEP-s'n-flaysh (kawt-LEH-t'n, GOO-lahsh).

620. Liver and onions.

לעבער מיט ציבעלעס׃

LEH-behr mit TSIB-eh-less.

621. Noodle pudding.

לאָקשן-קוגל׃

LAWK-sh'n-koo-g'l.

622. Omelette.

אָמלעט׃

awm-LET.

523. Pancakes (potato, matzo).

לאטקעס (קארטאָפֿל, מצה)·

LAHT-kes (kahr-TAW-f'l, MAH-tseh).

624. Pastrami.

פּאַסטראַמי·

pahst-RAH-mee.

625. Pirogen.

פּיראָגן·

pee-RAW-g'n.

626. Pot roast.

ראָסלפֿלייש·

RAW-s'l-flaysh.

627. Ribsteak.

ריפּנסטייק·

RIP'n-steak.

628. Salmon.

לאַקס·

lahx.

629. Sour cream and vegetables.

סמעטענע מיט גרינסן·

SMEH-teh-neh mit GREEN-s'n.

630. Tongue.

צונג·

tsoongg.

631. Turkey.

אינדיק·

IN-dik.

632. Veal chops.

קעלבערנע קאָטלעטן·

KEL-behr-neh kawt-LEH-t'n.

633. Whitefish.
וויסער פיש·
VI-sehr FISH.

FRUITS AND NUTS

634. Apple.
עפּל·
EH-p'l.

635. Bananas.
באַנאַנעס·
bah-NAH-nes.

636. Berries.
יאַגדעס·
YAHG-des.

637. Cherries.
קאַרשן·
KAHR-sh'n.

638. Fruit.
אויבס·
oyps.

639. Grapes.
ווינטרויבן·
VIN-troy-b'n.

640. Peaches.
פּערשקעס·
FEHRSH-kes.

641. Pears.
באַרנעס·
BAHR-nes.

642. Pineapples.
אַנאַנאַסן·
ah-nah-NAH-s'n.

643. Plums.
פֿלוימען.
FLOY-men.

644. Prunes.
געטריקנטע פֿלוימען.
geh-TRIK'n-teh FLOY-men.

645. Raisins.
ראָזשינקעס.
RAW-zhin-kes.

646. Almonds.
מאַנדלען.
MAHND-len.

647. Filberts.
וואַלדניס.
VAHLD-nis.

648. Nuts.
ניס.
nis.

649. Peanuts.
ערדניסלעך.
EHRD-nis-lekh.

650. Pecans.
פּיקאַנען.
pee-KAH-nen.

651. Walnuts.
וועלישע ניס.
VEH-lee-sheh NIS.

BEVERAGES

652. Coffee.
קאַװע (שװאַרצע).
KAH-veh (SHVAHR-tseh).

653. Coffee with milk (cream).
קאווע מיט מילך (שמאנט)·
KAH-veh mit MILKH (SHMAHNT).

654. Cocoa.
קאַקאַאָ·
kah-KAH-aw.

655. Lemonade.
לימאָנאַד·
lee-maw-NAHD.

656. Milk.
מילך·
MILKH.

657. Orangeade.
אראַנזשאַד·
aw-rahn-ZHAHD.

658. Seltzer.
סעלצער־וואַסער·
SEL-tsehr-vah-sehr.

659. Soda.
סאָדע·
SAW-deh.

660. Tea (with lemon).
טיי (מיט לימענע)·
TAY (mit LIM-eh-neh).

SEASONINGS

661. Chicken fat.
הינערשע שמאַלץ·
HEE-nehr-sheh SHMAHLTS.

662. Garlic.
קנאָבל·
K'NAW-b'l.

663. Horseradish.
כריין·
khrayn.

664. Ketchup.
קעטשאָפּ.
KETCH-up.

665. Mustard.
זענעפֿט.
ZEH-neft.

666. Oil.
בוימל.
BOY-m'l.

667. Pepper.
פֿעפֿער
FEH-fehr.

668. Salt.   **669. Sauce.**
זאַלץ.   סאָוס.
zahlts.   *souce.*

670. Granulated sugar.
מעלצוקער.
MEL-tsoo-kehr.

671. (Lump) sugar.
(האַרטער) צוקער.
(HAR-tehr) TSOO-kehr.

672. Vinegar.
עסיק.
EH-sik.

DESSERTS

673. Baked apple.
געבאַקענער עפּל.
geh-BAH-keh-nehr EH-p'l.

674. **Cheese cake.**
קעזקוכן·
KEZ-koo-kh'n.

675. **Coffee cake.**
קאַװע־קוכן·
KAH-veh-koo-kh'n.

676. **Honey cake.**
האָניק־לעקעך·
HAW-nik-leh-kekh.

677. **Sponge cake.**
טאָרט·
tawrt.

678. **Cookies.**
קיכעלעך·
KEE-kheh-lekh.

679. **Stewed fruit.**
קאָמפּאָט·
kawm-PAWT.

680. **Ice cream.**
אײזקרעם·
IZ-krem.

681. **Pastry.**
געבעקס·
geh-BEKS.

682. **Pie.**
פּײ·
pi.

683. **Rice pudding.**
רײזקוגל·
RIZ-koo-g'l.

684. Sherbet.

פרוקטאיז·

FROOKHT-Iz.

685. Strudel.

שטרודל·

SHTROO-d'l.

PLACES OF WORSHIP

686. A synagogue.

א שול·

ah SHOOL.

687. Where is there a service in English?

וואו איז מען מתפלל אויף ענגליש?

VOO iz men mis-PAH-lel oyf ENGG-lish?

688. When can we pray?

ווען דאוונט מען?

VEN DAH-v'nt men?

689. The services are orthodox (conservative, re-formed).

דער נוסח איז אן ארטאדאקסישער (קאנסער־
וואטיווער, רעפארמירטער)·

*dehr NOO-sahkh iz ahn or-taw-DAWK-see-shehr
(kawn-sehr-vah-TEE-vehr, reh-for-MEER-tehr).*

690. Is there an English-speaking rabbi?

צי איז פאראן א רב וואס רעדט ענגליש?

tsee iz fah-RAHN ah RAWV vaws RET ENGG-lish?

691. Is Hebrew (Yiddish) taught in (the religious) school?

צי לערנט מען העברעיש (ייריש) אין (דער
רעליגיעזער) שול?

*tsee LEH-r'nt men heb-RAY-ish (YEE-dish) in (dehr
reh-leeg-YEH-zehr) SHOOL?*

692. The wedding.

די חתונה·

dee KHAH-seh-neh.

693. The Bar Mitsvah.

די בר־מיצוה·

dee bahr-MITS-veh.

SIGHTSEEING

694. I want to hire a car.

איך וויל דינגען אן אויטא·

eekh vil DIN-gen ahn OY-taw.

695. I want a guide who speaks English.

איך דארף א פירער וואָס רעדט ענגליש·

eekh DAHRF ah FEE-rehr vaws RET ENGG-lish.

696. Call for me tomorrow at my hotel at 9 o'clock.

נעמט מיך מארגן אָפּ אין מיין האָטעל נין א
זייגער·

NEMT mikh MOR-g'n AWP in min haw-TEL NIN ah ZAY-gehr.

697. What is the charge per hour (per day)?

וויפל קאָסט א שעה (א טאָג)?

VEE-f'l COST ah SHAW (ah TAWG)?

698. How much do you want for the whole trip?

וויפל פאַרלאַנגט איר פאַר דער גאַנצער
ריזע?

VEE-f'l far-LAHNKT eer fahr dehr GAHN-tsehr RI-zeh?

699. Please show me all the sights of interest.

זייט אזוי גוט· וויזט מיר אַלץ וואָס איז
טשיקאַוועה צו זען·

ZIT ah-zoy GOOT, VIST meer AHLTS vaws iz chee-KAH-veh tsoo ZEN.

700. I wish to take a sightseeing trip around the city.

איך וויל ארומפֿאָרן באַקוקן די שטאָט.

eekh VIL ah-ROOM-faw-r'n bah-KOO-k'n dee SHTAWT.

701. Native arts and crafts.   **702.** Architecture.

אַרטיקע האַנטאַרבעטס.   אַרכיטעקטור.

OR-tee-keh HAHNT-ahr-bet.   *ahr-khee-tek-TOOR.*

703. Painting.   **704.** Sculpture.   **705.** Ruins.

מאָלערײַ.   סקולפּטור   רוינעס.

maw-leh-RI.   *skoolp-TOOR*   *roo-EE-nes.*

706. Shall I have time to visit the museums?

צי וועט מיר קלעקן צײַט צו באַזוכן די מוזייען?

tsee vet meer KLEH-k'n TSIT tsoo bah-ZOO-kh'n dee moo-ZAY-en?

707. How long does it take to walk?

ווי לאַנג געדויערט צוצוגיין?

vee LAHNGG geh-DOY-ehrt TSOO-tsoo-gayn?

708. Is it (still) open?

צי איז עס (נאָך) אָפֿן?

tsee iz es (nawkh) AW-f'n?

709. How long does it stay open?

ווי לאַנג בלײַבט עס אָפֿן?

vee LAHNGG BLIPT es AW-f'n?

710. We want to stop for refreshments.

מיר ווילן זיך אָפּשטעלן אויף איבערצוביסן.

meer VIL'n zikh AWP-shteh-l'n oyf EE-behr-tsoo-bi̇-s'n.

711. How long must I wait?

ווי לאַנג מוז איך וואַרטן?

vee LAHNGG mooz eekh VᴬHR-t'n?

712. Where is the entrance (the exit)?

וואו איז דער אַרײַנגאַנג (דער אַרויסגאַנג)?

VOO iz dehr ah-RIN-gahngg (dehr ah-ROYS-gahngg)?

713. What is the price of admission?

וויפֿל קאָסט אַרײַנצוגיין?

VEE-f'l COST ah-RIN-tsoo-gayn?

714. Do we need an interpreter?

צי דאַרפֿן מיר אָן איבערזעצער?

tsee DAHR-f'n meer ahn EE-behr-zeh-tsehr?

715. How much is the guidebook?

וויפֿל קאָסט דאָס פֿירערביכל?

VEE-f'l COST daws FEE-rehr-bee-kh'l?

716. May I take photographs?

צי מעג איך פֿאָטאָגראַפֿירן?

tsee MEG eekh faw-tawg-rah-FEE-r'n?

717. We want to stop for postcards (souvenirs).

מיר ווילן זיך אָפּשטעלן קויפֿן פּאָסטקאַרטלעך
(אָנדענקונגען).

meer VIL'n zikh AWP-shteh-l'n KOY-f'n PAWST-kahrt-lekh (AWN-den-koon-gen).

718. Do you have a book in English about ——?

צי האָט איר אַ בוך אויף ענגליש וועגן ——?

tsee HAWT eer ah BOOKH oyf ENGG-lish veh-g'n ——?

719. Take me back to the hotel.

פֿירט מיך אָפּ אין האָטעל.

FEERT mikh AWP in haw-TEL.

720. Go back by way of the business section.

פֿאָרט צוריק דורכן געשעפֿט-קוואַרטאַל.

FAWRT tsoo-RIK door-kh'n geh-SHEFT-kvahr-tahl.

ENTERTAINMENT

721. Where can we go to dance?

וואו קענען מיר גיין טאַנצן?

VOO keh-nen meer GAYN TAHN-ts'n?

722. May I have this dance?

צי קען איך איך בעטן צו דעם טאַנץ?

tsee KEN eekh ikh BEH-t'n tsoo DEM TAHNTS?

723. Is there a matinee today?

צי קומט הײַנט פֿאַר אַ מאַטינע?

tsee KOOMT hint FOR ah mah-tee-NEH?

724. When does the evening performance (floor-show) start?

ווען הייבט זיך אָן די אָוונט־פֿאָרשטעלונג (קאַבאַרע־פֿאָרשטעלונג)?

VEN HAYPT zikh AWN dee AW-v'nt-for-shteh-loongg (kah-bah-REH-for-shteh-loongg)?

725. Please play a foxtrot (rumba, tango, waltz, hora, sher).

שפּילט, זײַט אַזוי גוט, אַ פֿאָקסטראָט (רומבאַ, טאַנגאַ, וואַלץ, הורה, שער),

SHPEELT, ZIT ah-zoy GOOT, ah fawks-TRAWT (ROOM-bah, TAHN-gaw, VAHLTS, HAW-reh, SHEHR).

726. Have you any seats for tonight?

צי האָט איר ערטער אויף הײַנט אין אָוונט?

tsee HAWT eer EHR-tehr oyf HINT in AW-v'nt?

727. Can I see (hear) well from there?

צי קען איך פֿון דאָרטן גוט זען (הערן)?

tsee KEN eekh foon DOR-t'n GOOT ZEN (HEH-r'n)?

728. Not too near (far).

ניט צו נאָענט (ווייט)·

NIT TSOO NAW-ent (VIT).

729. The music is excellent.

די מוזיק איז אויסגעצייכנט·

dee moo-ZIK iz OYS-geh-TSAY-kh'nt.

730. This is very interesting (funny).

דאָס איז זייער אינטערעסאַנט (קאָמיש)·

DAWS eez ZAY-ehr in-teh-reh-SAHNT (KAW-mish).

731. Is this the intermission?

צי איז דאָס די הפסקה?

tsee iz DAWS dee hahf-SAW-keh?

732. The balcony.

דער באַלקאָן·

dehr bahl-KAWN.

733. The ballet.

דער באַלעט·

dehr bah-LET.

734. The beach.

דער פּליאַזש·

dehr PLAHZH.

735. The box.

די לאָזשע·

dee LAW-zheh.

736. The box office.

די קאַסע·

dee KAH-seh.

737. The café.

דער קאַפע·

dehr kah-FEH.

738. The concert.
דער קאָנצערט.
dehr kawn-TSEHRT.

739. The cover charge.
דער גענעראַלער אָפּצאָל.
dehr geh-neh-RAH-lehr AWP-tsawl.

740. The folk dances.
די פֿאָלקסטענץ.
dee FAWLKS-tents.

741. The gambling casino.
דער אַזאַרט־קאַסינאָ.
dehr ah-ZART-kah-see-naw.

742. The minimum.
דער מינימום.
dehr MEE-nee-moom.

743. The movies.
דער קינאָ.
dehr KEE-naw.

744. The night club.
דער נאַכטלאָקאַל.
dehr NAHKHT-law-kahl.

745. The opera.
די אָפּערע.
dee AW-peh-reh.

746. The opera glasses.
דער בינאָקל.
dehr bee-NAW-k'l.

747. The orchestra seat.
דער פֿאָרטערפּלאַץ.
dehr puhr TEHR-plahts.

748. The program.
די פּראָגראַם.
dee praw-GRAHM.

749. The reserved seat.
דער רעזערווירטער אָרט.
dehr reh-zehr-VEER-tehr ORT.

750. The theatre.
דער טעאַטער.
dehr teh-AH-tehr.

SPORTS

751. Baseball.
בייסבאָל.
BAYS-bahl.

752. Fishing.
כאַפּן פֿיש.
KHAH-p'n FISH.

753. Foot ball.
פֿוסבאָל.
FOOS-bahl.

754. Golf.
גאָלף.
gawlf.

755. The golf clubs.
די גאָלפֿשטעקנס.
dee GAWLF-shteh-k'ns.

756. The horse races.
די פֿערדגעיעגן.
dee FEHRD-geh-yeh-g'n.

757. Skating.
גליטשן זיך.
GLICH'n zikh.

758. Skiing.

נאַרטלען זיך.

NAHRT-len zikh.

759. Tennis.

טעניס.

TEH-nis.

SCHOOL

760. I am a student at —— school.

איך בין אַ תּלמיד אין דער —— שול.

eekh bin ah TAHL-mid in dehr —— SHOOL.

761. I wish to improve my ——.

איך וויל זיך פֿאַרבעסערן אויף——.

eekh VIL zikh fahr-BEH-seh-r'n oyf ——.

762. Can you direct me to a day school (night school)?

צי קענט איר מיר אָנוויזן אַ טאָגשול (אָוונטשול)?

tsee KENT eer meer AWN-vî-z'n ah TAWG-shool (AW-v'nt-shool)?

763. I wish to graduate with a high school diploma.

איך וויל גראַדוירן מיט אַ מיטלשול־דיפּלאָם.

eekh VIL grah-doo-EE-r'n mit ah MIT'l-shool-dip-lawm.

764. Is it free?

צי איז עס אומזיסט?

tsee iz es oom-ZIST?

765. My children are studying ——.

מײַנע קינדער לערנען——.

mî-neh KIN-dehr LEHR-nen ——.

766. I am a teacher of English.

איך בין אַן ענגליש־לערער·

eekh bin ahn ENGG-lish-leh-rehr.

767. Where is the public library?

וואו איז די עפֿנטלעכע ביבליאָטעק?

VOO iz dee EH-f'nt-leh-kheh bib-lee-aw-TEK?

SCHOOLS

768. The nursery school.

דער פּראַ־קינדער־גאָרטן·

dehr PRAW-KIN-dehr-gawr-t'n.

769. The kindergarten.

דער קינדער־גאָרטן·

dehr KIN-dehr-gawr-t'n.

770. The elementary school.

די עלעמענטאַר־שול·

dee eh-leh-men-TAHR-shool.

771. The junior high school.

די פּראַ־מיטלשול·

dee PRAW-MIT'l-shool.

772. The high school.

די מיטלשול·

dee MIT'l-shool.

773. The trade school.

די פֿאַכשול·

dee FAHKH-shool.

774. The college.

דער קאָלעדזש·

dehr KAH-ledzh.

775. The university.
דער אוניווערסיטעט.
dehr oo-nee-vehr-see-TET.

776. The heder.
דער חדר.
dehr KHAY-dehr.

777. The Hebrew school.
די העברעישע שול, די תלמוד־תורה.
dee heb-REH-ee-sheh SHOOL, dee tahl-mood-TOY-reh.

778. The Yiddish school.
די יידישע שול.
dee YEE-dee-sheh SHOOL.

779. The Yeshiva.
די ישיבה.
dee yeh-SHEE-veh.

SUBJECTS

780. Arithmetic.
אריטמעטיק.
ah-rit-MEH-tik.

781. Art.
קונסט.
KOONST.

782. Chemistry.
כעמיע.
KHEM-yeh.

783. Economics.
עקאנאמיק.
eh-kaw-NAW-mik.

784. English.
ענגליש.
ENGG-lish.

785. History.
געשיכטע·
geh-SHIKH-teh.

786. Languages.
שפראכן·
SHPRAH-kh'n.

787. Mathematics.
מאטעמאטיק·
mah-teh-MAH-tik.

788. Music.
מוזיק·
moo-ZIK.

789. Philosophy.
פילאסאפיע·
fee-law-SAWF-yeh.

790. Physics.
פיזיק·
fee-ZIK.

791. Reading.
לייענען·
LAY-eh-nen.

792. Social studies.
סאציאלע לימודים·
sawts-YAH-leh lee-MOO-dim.

793. Spelling.
אויסלייג·
OYS-layg.

PROFESSIONS

794. The actor.
דער אקטיאר·
dehr ahkt-YAWR.

795. The actress.
די אקטריסע·
dee ahkt-RIS-eh.

796. The artist.
דער קינסטלער•
dehr KINST-lehr.

797. The broker.
דער מעקלער•
dehr MEK-lehr.

798. The banker.
דער באנקיר•
dehr bahn-KEER.

799. The chemist.
דער כעמיקער•
dehr KHEH-mee-kehr.

800. The dancer.
דער טענצער•
dehr TEN-tsehr.

801. The dentist.
דער צאנדאקטער•
dehr TSAWN-dawk-tehr.

802. The doctor.
דער דאקטער•
dehr DAWK-tehr.

803. The engineer.
דער אינושעניר•
dehr in-zheh-NEER.

804. The journalist.
דער זשורנאליסט•
dehr zhoor-nah-LIST.

805. The lawyer.
דער אדוואקאט•
dehr ahd-vaw-KAHT.

806. The musician.
דער מוזיקער•
dehr MOO-zee-kehr.

807. The oculist.
דער אויגן־דאָקטער•
dehr OY-g'n-dawk-tehr.

808. The optometrist.
דער אָפּטיקער•
dehr AWP-tee-kehr.

809. The pharmacist.
דער אַפּטייקער•
dehr ahp-TAY-kehr.

810. The printer.
דער דרוקער•
dehr DROO-kehr.

811. The scientist.
דער װיסנשאַפֿטלער•
dehr VIS'n-shahft-lehr.

812. The surgeon.
דער כירורג•
dehr khee-ROORG.

813. The teacher.
דער לערער•
dehr LEH-rehr.

EMPLOYMENT

814. I am looking for a job.
איך זוך אַ שטעלע•
eekh ZOOKH ah SHTEH-leh.

815. These are my references.
אָט זײַנען מײַנע רעפֿערענצן•
AWT zĭ-nen mĭ-neh reh-feh-REN-ts'n.

816. Mr. —— sent me to you.
הער —— האָט מיך צו איך געשיקט•
hehr —— hawt meekh tsoo ĬKH geh-shikt.

817. **I worked with this company for —— years.**

איך האָב געאַרבעט ביַ דער פֿירמע —— יאָר.

eekh hawb geh-AHR-bet bĭ dehr FEER-meh ——
YAWR.

818. **I am a mechanic by trade.**

איך בין אַ מעכאַניקער פֿון פֿאַך.

eekh bin ah meh-KHAH-nee-kehr foon FAHKH.

819. **I am a graduate of —— school.**

איך בין אַ גראַדואַנט פֿון דער —— שול.

eekh been ah grah-doo-AHNT foon dehr —— SHOOL.

820. **I have a diploma.**

איך האָב אַ דיפּלאָם.

eekh HAWB ah dip-LAWM.

821. **I can start at once.**

איך קען תּיכּף אָנהייבן.

eekh KEN TAY-kef AWN-hay-b'n.

822. **The salary is satisfactory.**

די שׂכירות שטעלן מיך צופֿרידן.

dee SKHEE-res SHTEH-l'n meekh tsoo-FREE-d'n.

823. **Where can I get a social security card?**

וואו קען איך קריגן אַ קאַרטל פֿאַר דער
סאָציאַלער פֿאַרזיכערונג?

VOO ken eekh KRIG'n ah KAHR-t'l fahr dehr sawts-
YAH-lehr fahr-ZEE-kheh-roongg?

WORD LIST

824. **The apprentice.**

דאָס לערנינגל.

daws LEH-r'n-yin-g'l.

825. **The baker.**

דער בעקער.

dehr BEH-kehr.

826. The carpenter.

דער סטאַליער־

dehr STAWL-yehr.

827. The compensation.

די פֿאַרגיטיקונג־

dee fahr-GEE-tee-koongg.

828. The civil service.

די ציווילדינסט־

dee tsee-VEEL-deenst.

829. The classified ad.

דער קלאַסיפֿיצירטער אַנאַנס־

dehr klah-see-fee-TSEER-tehr ah-NAWNS.

830. The cutter.

דער צושנײַדער־

dehr TSOO-shni-dehr.

831. The designer.

דער מאָדעלן־צײַכענער־

dehr maw-DEH-l'n-tsay-kheh-nehr.

832. The dues.

דער אָפּצאָל־

dehr AWP-tsawl.

833. Employ.

אַנשטעלן

AWN-shteh-l'n.

834. The employee.

דער אַנעשטעלטער־

dehr AWN-geh-shtel-tehr.

835. The employer.

דער אַרבעט־געבער־

dehr AHR-bet-geh-behr.

836. The employment agency.

די אַרבעט־אַגענטור־

dee AHR-bet-ah-gen-toor.

837. The electrician.

דער עלעקטריקער־

dehr eh-LEK-tree-kehr.

838. The experience.

די פּראָקטיק.

dee PRAHK-tik.

839. The foreman.

דער אויפֿזעער.

dehr OYF-zeh-ehr.

840. The helper.

דער געהילף.

dehr geh-HILF.

841. The income tax.

דער הכנסה־שטײַער.

dehr hahkh-NAW-seh-shtī-ehr.

842. The mechanic.

דער מעכאַניקער.

dehr meh-KHAH-nee-kehr.

843. The meeting.

די פֿאַרזאַמלונג.

dee fahr-ZAHM-loongg.

844. The plumber.

דער רערן־שלאָסער.

dehr REH-r'n-shlaw-sehr.

845. The profession.

די פּראָפֿעסיע.

dee praw-FES-yeh.

846. The position.

די שטעלע.

dee SHTEH-leh.

847. The salary.

די שכירות.

dee SKHEE-res.

848. The salesman.

דער פֿאַרקויפֿער.

dehr fahr-KOY-fehr.

849. The storekeeper.

דער קרעמער.

dehr KREH-mehr.

850. The tailor.

דער שנײַדער•

dehr SHNÍ-dehr.

851. The technician.

דער טעכניקער•

dehr TEKH-nee-kehr.

852. The tool maker.

דער מכשירים־מאַכער

dehr mahkh-SHEE-rim-mah-khehr.

853. The trade.

דער פֿאַך•

dehr FAHKH.

854. The union.

דער פֿאַראײן•

dehr fahr-AYN.

855. The wage.

דער לוין•

dehr LOYN.

856. The work.

די אַרבעט•

dee AHR-bet.

857. The worker.

דער אַרבעטער•

dehr AHR-beh-tehr.

BANK AND MONEY

858. Where is the nearest bank?

װאָו איז דער נאָענטסטער באַנק?

voo iz dehr NAW-ents-tehr BAHNK?

859. Where is the nearest branch of this bank?

װאָו איז די נאָענטסטע פֿיליאַלע פֿון דעם באַנק?

VOO iz dee NAW-ents-teh feel-YAH-leh foon DEM BAHNK?

860. When does the bank open (close)?

ווען עפֿנט (פֿארמאכט) זיך דער באַנק?

VEN EH-f'nt (fahr-MAHKHT) zikh dehr BAHNK?

861. Give me (do not give me) large bills.

גיט מיר (גיט מיר ניט קיין) גרויסע באַנקנאָטן.

GIT meer (GIT meer NIT kayn) GROY-seh bahnk-NAW-t'n.

862. May I have some change?

צי קענט איר מיר געבן קליינגעלט?

tsee KENT eer meer GEH-b'n KLAYN-gelt?

863. At which window can I cash this?

בײַ וועלכן פֿענצטער קען איך עס אײַנקאַסירן?

bī VEL-kh'n FENTS-tehr KEN eekh es IN-kah-see-r'n?

864. Can you change this for me?

צי קענט איר מיר עס אויסבײַטן?

tsee KENT eer meer es OYS-bī-t'n?

865. I want to send fifty dollars to ——.

איך וויל שיקן פֿופֿציק דאָלאַר קיין——.

eekh vil SHIK'n FOOF-tsik DAW-lahr kayn ——.

866. What is the exchange rate on the dollar?

וויפֿל איז דער קורס פֿון דאָלאַר?

VEE-f'l iz dehr KOORS foon DAW-lahr?

867. I have traveler's checks.

איך האָב רײַזעטשעקן.

eekh HAWB RĪ-zeh-cheh-k'n.

868. I want to open a checking account.

איך וויל עפֿענען אַ טשעקקאָנטע.

eekh VIL EH-feh-nen ah CHECK-kawn-teh.

869. I have a letter of credit from this bank.

איך האָב אַ קרעדיטבריוו פֿון דעם באַנק.

eekh HAWB ah kreh-DIT-breev foon DEM BAHNK.

870. I wish to buy a draft on ——.

איך װיל קױפֿן אַ טראַטע אױף——·

eekh VIL KOY-f'n ah TRAH-teh oyf——.

871. Can you cash an American Express check?

צי קענט איר אײַנקאַסירן אַ טשעק פֿון אַמעריקען עקספּרעס?

tsee KENT eer IN-kah-see-r'n ah CHECK foon ah-MER-i-kan eks-PRES?

872. May I have a check book?

צי קענט איר מיר געבן אַ טשעקביכל?

tsee KENT eer meer GEH-b'n ah CHECK-bee-kh'l?

873. Please cash this check for me.

זײַט אַזױ גוט, קאַסירט מיר אין דעם טשעק·

ZIT ah-zoy GOOT, kah-SEERT meer IN DEM CHECK.

874. Let me have a statement of my account.

גיט מיר אַן אױסצוג פֿון מײַן קאָנטע·

GIT meer ahn OYS-tsoog foon mīn KAWN-teh.

875. What is my balance?

װיפֿל באַטרעפֿט מײַן באַלאַנס?

VEE-f'l bah-TREFT mīn bah-LAHNS?

876. We cannot give you any credit.

מיר קענען אײַך קײן קרעדיט ניט געבן·

meer KEH-nen īkh kayn kreh-DIT nit GEH-b'n.

877. Let me have some notes and silver.

גיט מיר באַנקנאָטן און מינץ·

GEET meer bahnk-NAW-t'n oon MINTS.

878. Please pay my current bills.

זײַט אַזױ גוט, באַצאָלט מײַנע לױפֿיקע רעכענונגען·

ZIT ah-zoy GOOT, bah-TSAWLT mī-neh LOY-fee-keh REH-kheh-noon-gen.

879. When was the bill of exchange due?

ווען איז דער אויסבײט־צעטל געווען פֿעליק?

VEN iz dehr OYS-bit-tseh-t'l geh-VEN FEH-lik?

880. This check is payable to the bearer.

דעם טשעק דארף מען אויסצאָלן דעם וואָס
ברענגט אים.

*DEM CHECK dahrf men OYS-tsaw-l'n DEM vaws
BRENGT im.*

881. He has a good reputation.

ער האָט אַ גוטן שם.

ehr HAWT ah GOO-t'n SHEM.

BANKING: USEFUL WORDS

882. The account.

די קאָנטע.

dee KAWN-teh.

883. The bank (bank note).

דער באַנק (באַנקנאָט).

dehr BAHNK (bahnk-NAWT).

884. The bearer.

דער ברענגער.

dehr BREN-gehr.

885. The bonds.

די אָבליגאַציעס.

dee awb-lee-GAHTS-yes.

886. The branch.

די פֿיליאַלע.

dee feel-YAH-leh.

887. The cash.

דאָס מזומן.

daws meh-ZOO-men.

888. The cashier.

דער קאַסירער.

dehr kah-SEE-rehr.

889. The (certified) check.
דער (סערטיפיצירטער) טשעק•
dehr (sehr-tee-fee-TSEER-tehr) CHECK.

890. The credit.
דער קרעדיט•
dehr kreh-DIT.

891. The creditor.
דער קרעדיטאָר•
dehr kreh-DIT-or.

892. The debit.
דער דעבעט•
dehr DEH-bet.

893. The debt.
דער חוב•
dehr KHOYV.

894. The debtor.
דער בעל־חוב•
dehr bahl-KHOYV.

895. The draft.
די טראַטע•
dee TRAH-teh.

896. Endorse.
זשערירן•
zheh-REE-r'n.

897. The endorser.
דער זשערירער•
dehr zheh-REE-rehr.

898. The exchange.
דער אויסבמיט•
dehr OYS-bit.

899. The I.O.U.
דער וועקסל•
dehr VEK-s'l.

900. The interest.
ער פּראָצענט•
dehr praw-TSENT.

901. The letter of credit.

דער קרעדיטבריװ•

dehr kreh-DIT-breev.

902. The loan.

די הלװאה•

dee hahl-VAW-eh.

903. The (personal) note.

דער (פערזענלעכער) װעקסל•

dehr (pehr-ZEN-leh-khehr) VEK-s'l.

904. The security.

די גאראנטיע•

dee gah-RAHNT-yeh.

905. The share.

די אקציע•

dee AHKTS-yeh.

906. The shareholder.

דער אקציאנער•

dehr ahkts-yaw-NEHR.

907. The signature.

די אונטערשריפט•

dee 'OON-tehr-shrift.

908. The statement.

דער קאנטע־אויסצוג•

dehr KAWN-teh-oys-tsoog.

909. The stockbroker.

דער מעקלער•

dehr MEK-lehr.

BUSINESS

910. Where is the buying office?

װאו איז דאס איינקויף־ביורא?

VOO iz daws !N-koyf-bew-raw?

911. I wish to speak to the buyer.

איך װיל רעדן מיטן איינקויפער•

eekh VIL REH-d'n mit'n IN-koy-fehr.

912. Please tell him I will call back.

זײַט אַזױ גוט, זאָגט אים, אַז איך װעל צוריק־
קלינגען.

ZIT ah-zoy GOOT, ZAWKT eem, ahz eekh vel tsoo-
RIK-klin-gen.

913. I am staying at ——.

איך שטײ אין אין ——.

eekh SHTAY IN in ——.

914. Here is my card.

אָט איז מײַן װיזיט־קאַרטל.

AWT iz mïn vee-ZIT-kahr-t'l.

915. He is expecting my arrival.

ער ריכט זיך אױף מיר.

ehr REEKHT zikh oyf meer.

916. I have a letter of introduction.

איך האָב אַ רעקאָמענדיר־בריװ.

eekh hawb ah reh-kaw-men-DEER-breev.

917. When will he (she) be in the office?

װען װעט ער (זי) זײַן אין ביוראָ?

VEN vet ehr (zee) ZIN in bew-RAW?

918. I want to arrange an appointment.

איך װיל באַשטעלן אַ צונױפֿטרעף.

eekh VIL bah-SHTEH-l'n ah tsoo-NOYF-tref.

919. It is important.

עס איז װיכטיק.

es iz VEEKH-tik.

920. I have some new samples to show you.

איך האָב ניִע מוסטערן אײַך צו װײַזן.

eekh HAWB NI-eh MOOS-teh-r'n ïkh tsoo VI-z'n.

921. I represent —— company.

איך רעפּרעזענטיר די געזעלשאַפֿט ——.

eekh rep-reh-zen-TEER dee geh-ZEL-shahft ——.

922. We manufacture, sell, distribute.

מיר פֿאַבריצירן, פֿאַרקױפֿן, פֿאַרשפּרײטן.

meer fahb-ree-TSEE-r'n, fahr-KOY-f'n, fahr-SHPRAY-t'n.

923. These are our discounts.

דאָס זיינען אונדזערע הנחות.

DAWS zĭ-nen OON-dzeh-reh hah-NAW-khes.

924. You get a discount if you meet the bill.

איר קריגט אַ הנחה אױב איר באַצאָלט דעם חשבון פֿאַרן טערמין.

eer KRIKT ah hah-NAW-kheh OYB eer bah-TSAWLT dem KHESH-b'n FAH-r'n tehr-MEEN.

925. Our terms are as follows:

אונדזערע תּנאים זיינען אַזעלכע:

OON-dzeh-reh TNAW-im zĭ-nen ah-ZEL-kheh:

926. When can you confirm this order?

ווען קענט איר באַשטעטיקן די באַשטעלונג?

VEN kent eer bah-SHTEH-tee-k'n DEE bah-SHTEH-loongg?

927. We pay our salemen a 10% commission.

מיר צאָלן אונדזערע פֿאַרקױפֿערס צען פּראָצענט קאָמיסיע.

meer TSAW-l'n oon-dzeh-reh fahr-KOY-fehrs TSEN praw-TSENT kaw-MIS-yeh.

928. Ship this order via ——.

שיקט די באַשטעלונג דורך ——.

SHIKT dee bah-SHTEH-loongg doorkh ——.

929. Delivery must be made by ——.

צושטעלן מוז מען ביז ——.

TSOO-shteh-l'n mooz men BEEZ ——.

930. This has been a good (slack) season for ——.

דאָס איז געווען אַ גוטער (שוואַכער) סעזאָן
אויף ——.

*DAWS iz geh-VEN ah GOO-tehr (SHVAH-khehr)
seh-ZAWN oyf ——.*

931. Our fall line will be ready in —— weeks.

אונדזער האַרבסטיקע סחורה וועט זיין פאַרטיק
אין —— וואָכן אַרום.

*oon-dzehr HAHRB-stee-keh SKHOY-reh vet ZIN
FAHR-tik in —— VAW-kh'n ah-ROOM.*

932. Here are our catalogues and price lists.

אָט זיינען אונדזערע קאַטאַלאָגן און פּריזן־
רשימות.

*AWT zi-nen oon-dzeh-reh kah-tah-LAW-g'n oon
PRI-z'n-reh-shee-mes.*

933. All prices are (not) subject to change.

אַלע פּריזן זיינען (ניט) עלול זיך צו ביטן.

AH-leh PRI-z'n zinen (NIT) AW-lel zikh tsoo BI-t'n.

934. Please confirm our conversation by letter.

זיט אַזוי גוט, באַשטעטיקט אונדזער שמועס
אין אַ בריוו.

*ZIT ah-zoy GOOT, bah-SHTEH-tikt oon-dzehr
SHMOO-es in ah BREEV.*

**935. I can send you an estimate on the cost of
equipment.**

איך קען איך שיקן אַ שאַצונג אויפן פּריז פון
דער אויסשטאַטונג.

*eekh ken ikh SHIK'n ah SHAH-tsoongg oy-f'n PRIZ
foon dehr OYS-shtah-toongg.*

936. We can promise delivery in —— days.

מיר קענען צוזאָגן עס צוצושטעלן אין —— טעג
אַרום.

meer keh-nen TSOO-zaw-g'n es TSOO-tsoo-shteh-l'n in —— TEG ah-ROOM.

937. Can I have copies made of these papers?

צי קען איך לאָזן קאָפּירן די פּאַפּירן?

tsee KEN eekh LAW-z'n kaw-PEE-r'n dee pah-PEE-r'n?

938. I expect to leave the city on ——.

איך רעכט זיך אָפּצופאָרן פֿון שטאָט ——.

eekh REEKHT zikh AWP-tsoo-faw-r'n foon SHTAWT ——.

939. I will leave my mailing address with your secretary.

איך וועל איבערלאָזן מיין פּאָסטאַדרעס בײַ
אײַער סעקרעטאַרשע.

eekh vel EE-behr-law-z'n mīn PAWST-ahd-res bī ī-ehr sek-reh-TAHR-sheh.

940. We can draw up and sign a contract later.

מיר קענען צונויפֿשטעלן און אונטערשרײַבן
אַ קאָנטראַקט שפּעטער.

meer keh-nen tsoo-NOYF-shteh-l'n oon OON-tehr-shrī-b'n ah kawn-TRAHKT SHPEH-tehr.

941. The firm is bankrupt.

די פֿירמע איז באַנקראָט.

dee FEER-meh iz bahnk-RAWT.

BUSINESS VOCABULARY

942. Accounts payable.

חשבונות צום אויסצאָלן.

khesh-BOY-nes tsoom OYS-tsaw-l'n.

943. Accounts receivable.

חשבונות צום אײנמאַנען∙

khesh-BOY-nes tsoom IN-maw-nen.

944. Advertising.

די רעקלאַמע∙

dee rek-LAH-meh.

945. The advertising manager.

דער רעקלאַמע־פֿאַרוואַלטער∙

dehr rek-LAH-meh-fahr-vahl-tehr.

946. The agent.

דער אַגענט∙

dehr ah-GENT.

947. The bill.

דער חשבון∙

dehr KHESH-b'n.

948. The bill of exchange.

דער אויסבײַט־צעטל∙

dehr OYS-bit-tseh-t'l.

949. The bill of lading.

דער לאָדצעטל∙

dehr LAWD-tseh-t'l.

950. The bill of sale.

דער פֿאַרקויף־צעטל∙

dehr far-KOYF-tseh-t'l.

951. The bookkeeper.

דער בוכהאַלטער∙

dehr bookh-HAHL-tehr.

952. The building.

דער בנין∙

dehr BIN-yen.

953. The business.

דאָס געשעפֿט∙

daws geh-SHEFT.

954. The buyer.

דער אײנקויפֿער∙

dehr IN-koy-fehr.

955. A cancellation.

אן אנולירונג׃

ahn ah-noo-LEE-roongg.

956. The catalogue.

דער קאטאלאג׃

dehr kah-tah-LAWG.

957. Commerce.

מיסחר׃

MEES-khehr.

958. The company.

די געזעלשאפט׃

dee geh-ZEL-shahft.

959. The conference.

די באראטונג׃

dee bah-RAH-toongg.

960. The contract.

דער קאנטראקט׃

dehr kawn-TRAHKT.

961. The consignment.

די שיקונג׃

dee SHEE-koongg.

962. The copy.

די קאפיע׃

dee KAWP-yeh.

963. Credit (long and short term).

דער קרעדיט (לאנג־ און קורץ־טערמיניקער)׃

dehr kreh-DIT (LAHNGG- oon KOORTS-tehr-mee-nee-kehr).

964. The delivery.

דער צושטעל׃

dehr TSOO-shtel.

965. The department.

דער אפטייל׃

dehr AWP-tayl.

966. The discount.

די הנחה׃

dee hah-NAW-kheh.

967. The document.
דער דאָקומענט.
dehr daw-koo-MENT.

968. The draft.
דער וועקסל.
dehr VEK-s'l.

969. The elevator.
דער ליפֿט.
dehr LIFT.

970. The chief engineer.
דער הויפּט־אינזשעניר.
dehr HOYPT-in-zheh-neer.

971. The estimate.
די שאַצונג.
dee SHAH-tsoongg.

972. The expert.
דער עקספּערט.
dehr ex-PEHRT.

973. For export.
אויף עקספּאָרט.
oyf ex-PAWRT.

974. Financial.
פֿינאַנציעל.
fee-nahnts-YEL.

975. The firm.
די פֿירמע.
dee FEER-meh.

976. Fully protected.
אין גאַנצן געשיצט.
in GAHN-ts'n geh-SHITST.

977. The freight.
די פֿראַכט.
dee FRAHKHT.

978. For import.
אויף אימפּאָרט.
oyf im-PAWRT.

979. The industry.

די אינדוסטריע.

dee in-DOOS-tree-eh.

980. The insurance.

די פֿאַרזיכערונג.

dee fahr-ZEE-kheh-roongg.

981. The invoice.

דער חשבון.

dehr KHESH-b'n.

982. The jobber.

דער פֿאַרמיטלער.

dehr fahr-MIT-lehr.

983. The lawyer.

דער אַדוואָקאַט.

dehr ahd-vaw-KAHT.

984. A letter of credit.

אַ קרעדיטבריוו.

ah kreh-DIT-breev.

985. The manager.

דער פֿאַרוואַלטער.

dehr fahr-VAHL-tehr.

986. The manufacturer.

דער פֿאַבריקאַנט.

dehr fahb-ree-KAHNT.

987. The messenger.

דער שליח.

dehr shaw-LEE-ahkh.

988. The model (style).

דער מאָדעל.

dehr maw-DEL.

989. The mannequin.

דער מאַנעקין.

dehr mah-neh-KEEN.

990. The mortgage.

די היפּאָטעק.

dee hee-paw-TEK.

991. The notary.
דער נאָטאַר.
dehr naw-TAHR.

992. The note.
דער וועקסל.
dehr VEK-s'l.

993. The office.
דאָס ביוראָ.
daws bew-RAW.

994. An option.
דאָס אָפּטירערעכט.
daws awp-TEER-rekht.

995. The down payment.
דער אָדערויף.
dehr AH-deh-royf.

996. The terms of payment.
די צאָל־תנאים.
dee TSAWL-tnaw-im.

997. Permission.
די דערלויבעניש.
dee dehr-LOY-beh-nish.

998. The power of attorney.
די פולמאַכט.
dee FOOL-mahkt.

999. The price.
דער פּריז.
dehr PRIZ.

1000. The price list.
די פּריזן־רשימה.
dee PRI-z'n-reh-shee-meh.

1001. The (net) profit.
דער (ריינער) ריווח.
dehr (RAY-nehr) REH-vahkh.

1002. The promissory note.
דער וועקסל.
dehr VEK-s'l.

1003. The promotion.
די פֿאַרשפּרייטונג׃
dee fahr-SHPRAY-toongg.

1004. The receptionist.
די אויפֿנעמערין׃
dee OYF-neh-meh-r'n.

1005. The representative.
דער פֿאָרשטייער׃
dehr FAWR-shtay-ehr.

1006. Retail.
לאַחדים׃
lah-KHAW-dim.

1007. Return for credit.
אומקערן אויף קרעדיט׃
OOM-keh-r'n oyf kreh-DEET.

1008. Returnable.
צום אומקערן׃
tsoom OOM-keh-r'n.

1009. The sale.
דער פֿאַרקויף׃
dehr fahr-KOYF.

1010. The salesman.
דער פֿאַרקויפֿער׃
dehr fahr-KOY-fehr.

1011. The sales manager.
דער פֿאַרקויף־פֿאַרוואַלטער׃
dehr fahr-KOYF-fahr-vahl-tehr.

1012. The samples.
די מוסטערן׃
dee MOOS-teh-r'n.

1013. The secretary.
די סעקרעטאַרשע׃
dee sek-reh-TAHR-sheh.

1014. The signature.
די אונטערשריפֿט׃
dee OON-tehr-shrift.

1015. The specialty store.

די ספּעציאַליטעט־קראָם׃

dee spets-yah-lee-TET-krawm.

1016. The stenographer.

די סטענאָגראַפֿיסטין׃

dee steh-nawg-rah-FIS-t'n.

1017. The territory.

די טעריטאָריע׃

dee teh-ree-TAWR-yeh.

1018. The trust.

דער טראָסט׃

dehr TRAWST.

1019. The typist.

די טיפּיסטין׃

dee tee-PIS-t'n.

1020. The typewriter.

די שרײַבמאַשין׃

dee SHRIB-mah-sheen.

1021. Wholesale.

הורט׃

hoort.

SHOPPING

1022. I want to go shopping.

איך וויל גיין אײַנקויפֿן׃

eekh VIL GAYN IN-koy-f'n.

1023. Please drive me around the shopping center.

זײַט אַזוי גוט׳ פֿירט מיך דורך דעם אײַנקויף־צענטער׃

ZIT ah-zoy GOOT, FEERT mikh doorkh dem IN-koyf-tsen-tehr.

1024. I am just looking around.

איך קוק זיך נאָר אַרום׃

eekh KOOK zikh NOR ah-ROOM.

1025. **May I speak to a male (female) sales clerk?**

צי קען איך רעדן מיט אַ פֿאַרקויפֿער
(פֿאַרקויפֿערין)?

*tsee KEN eekh REH-d'n mit ah fahr-KOY-fehr
(fahr-KOY-feh-r'n)?*

1026. **Is there an English-speaking person here?**

צי איז דאָ פֿאַראַן עמעצער װאָס רעדט ענגליש?

*tsee iz daw fah-RAHN EH-meh-tsehr vaws RET
ENGG-lish?*

1027. **Where is the bakery shop?**

װאו איז די בעקערײ?

VOO iz dee beh-keh-RI?

1028. **The antique shop.**

דאָס אַנטיק־געשעפֿט.

daws ahn-TIK'n-geh-sheft.

1029. **The bookshop.**

די ביכערקראָם.

dee BEE-khehr-krawm.

1030. **The candy store.**

די צוקערניע.

dee tsoo-KEHR-nveh.

1031. **The cigar store.**

די ציגאַרן־קראָם.

dee tsee-GAH-r'n-krawm.

1032. **The clothing store.**

די קלײדערקראָם.

dee KLAY-dehr-krawm.

1033. **The department store.**

די אוניװערסאַל־קראָם.

dee oo-nee-vehr-SAHL-krawm.

1034. The dressmaker.
די שניידערקע׃
dee SHNI-dehr-keh.

1035. The drug store.
די אַפּטייקקראָם׃
dee ahp-TAYK-krawm.

1036. The grocery.
די שפּייזקראָם׃
dee SHPIZ-krawm.

1037. The hardware store.
די אייזנוואַרג־קראָם׃
dee I-z'n-vahrg-krawm.

1038. The hat shop.
די הוטקראָם׃
dee HOOT-krawm.

1039. The jewelry store.
די צירונגקראָם׃
dee TSEE-roongg-krawm.

1040. The meat market.
דער פֿליישמאַרק׃
dehr FLAYSH-mahrk.

1041. The kosher butcher.
דער כּשרער קצבֿ׃
dehr KAW-sheh-rehr KAH-tsev.

1042. The shoe store.
די שוכקראָם׃
dee SHOOKH-krawm.

1043. The shoemaker.
דער שוסטער׃
dehr SHOOS-tehr.

1044. The tailor shop.

די שנײַדערײַ.

dee shnī-deh-RI.

1045. The toy shop.

די שפּילכלקראָם.

dee SHPEEL-kh'l-krawm.

1046. The watchmaker.

דער זײגער־מאַכער.

dehr ZAY-gehr-mah-khehr.

1047. Please regulate my watch for me.

זיט אַזױ גוט, רעגולירט מיר מײַן זײגער.

ZIT ah-zoy GOOT, reh-goo-LEERT meer mīn ZAY-gehr.

1048. How much will it cost to have it repaired?

וױפֿל װעט קאָסטן אים צו פֿאַרריכטן?

VEE-f'l vet KAWS-t'n eem tsoo fahr-REEKH-t'n?

1049. The sale.   **1050. The bargain.**

דער אױספֿאַרקױף.   די מציאה.

dehr OYS-fahr-koyf.   *dee meh-TSEE-eh.*

1051. I want to buy ——.

איך װיל קױפֿן ——.

eekh VIL KOY-f'n ——.

1052. How much is it (for each piece) altogether?

וױפֿל קאָסט (יעדער שטיק) אַלץ צחאַמען?

VEE-f'l COST (YEH-dehr SHTIK) AHLTS tsoo-ZAH-men?

1053. How much is it per yard?

וױפֿל קאָסט אַ יאָרד?

VEE-f'l COST ah YARD?

1054. It is very (too) expensive.

עס איז זײער (צו) טײַער.

es iz ZAY-ehr (TSOO) TI-ehr.

1055. You said it would cost ——.

איר האָט געזאָגט אַז עס וועט קאָסטן ——·

eer hawt geh-ZAWKT ahz es vet KAWS-t'n ——.

1056. I prefer something better (cheaper).

איך וואָלט וועלן עפּעס בעסערס (ביליקערס)·

eekh vawlt VEH-l'n eh-pes BEH-sehrs (BIL-ee-kehrs).

1057. Finer.

פֿײנערס·

FI-nehrs.

1058. Stronger.

שטאַרקערס·

SHTAHR-kehrs.

1059. Thicker.

גרעבערס·

GREH-behrs.

1060. Lighter.

לײכטערס·

LIKH-tehrs.

1061. Tighter.

ענגערס·

EN-gehrs.

1062. Looser.

לויזערס·

LOY-zehrs.

1063. Alike.

ענלעך·

EN-lekh.

1064. Different.

אַנדערש·

AHN-dehrsh.

1065. A pair.

אַ פּאָר·

ah PAWR.

1066. A dozen.

אַ טוץ·

ah TOOTS.

1067. Half a dozen.

אַ האַלבער טוץ·

ah HAHL-behr TOOTS.

1068. I do (not) like that.

מיר געפֿעלט דאָס (ניט)·

meer geh-FELT daws (nit).

1069. Show me some others.

ווײזט מיר אַנדערע·

VIST meer AHN-deh-reh.

1070. May I try this on?

צי קען איך דאָס אָנמעסטן?

tsee KEN eekh daws AWN-mes-t'n?

1017. Can I order one?

צי קען איך עס באַשטעלן?

tsee KEN eekh es bah-SHTEH-l'n?

1072. When shall I call for it?

ווען זאָל איך עס אָפּנעמען?

VEN zawl eekh es AWP-neh-men?

1073. How long will it take?

ווי לאַנג וועט עס געדויערן?

vee LAHNGG vet es geh-DOY-eh-r'n?

1074. Can you have it ready for this evening?

צי קענט איר עס האָבן גרייט אויף הינט אין
אָוונט?

*tsee KENT eer es haw-b'n GRAYT oyf HINT in
AW-v'nt?*

1075. Please take my measurements.

זײַט אַזוי גוט, נעמט פֿון מיר אַ מאָס.

ZIT ah-zoy GOOT, NEMT foon meer ah MAWS.

1076. It does (not) fit me.

עס פּאַסט מיר (ניט).

es PAHST meer (nit).

1077. It is (not) becoming to me.

עס קליידט מיר (ניט).

es KLAYT meer (nit).

1078. Will this fade (shrink)?

צי וועט עס אויסבלאַנקירן (אײַנציִען זיך)?

tsee vet es OYS-blahn-kee-r'n (IN-tsee-en zikh)?

1079. Wrap this, please.

פּאַקט עס אײַן, זײַט אַזוי גוט.

PAHKT es IN, ZIT ah-zoy GOOT.

1080. I will take it with me.

איך וויל עס מיטנעמען מיט זיך׃

eekh vil es MIT-neh-men mit ZEEKH.

1081. Can you ship it to me freight?

צי קענט איר מיר דאָס שיקן ווי פֿראַכט?

tsee KENT eer meer daws SHIK'n vee FRAHKHT?

1082. Whom do I pay?

וועמען זאָל איך באַצאָלן?

VEH-men zawl eekh vah-TSAW-l'n?

1083. Please bill me.

זיט אַזוי גוט׳ שיקט מיר אַ חשבון׃

ZIT ah-zoy GOOT, SHIKT meer ah KHESH-b'n.

1084. Are there any other charges (delivery charges)?

צי איז פֿאַראַן נאָך עפּעס אַן אָפּצאָל (צושטעל-אָפּצאָל)?

tsee eez fah-RAHN NAWKH eh-pes ahn AWP-tsawl (TSOO-shtel-awp-tsawl)?

1085. Let me have a sales slip.

גיט מיר אַ פֿאַרקויף-צעטל׃

GIT meer ah fahr-KOYF-tseh-t'l.

1086. You will be paid on delivery.

מען וועט אייך באַצאָלן ביים צושטעלן׃

men vet îkh bah-TSAW-l'n bîm TSOO-shteh-l'n.

1087. This parcel is fragile (perishable).

דאָס פּעקל קען זיך צעברעכן (קען קאַליע ווערן)׃

daws PEH-k'l KEN zikh tseh-BREH-kh'n (ken KAHL-veh veh-r'n).

1088. Pack this carefully for export.

פֿאַקט דאָס פֿאָרזיכטיק אין צום עקספּאָרטירן·

PAHKT daws FOR-zikh-tik IN tsoom ex-por-TEE-r'n.

CLOTHING

1089. An apron.

אַ פֿאָרטעך·

ah FAHR-tekh.

1090. A bathing cap.

אַ באָדהיטל·

ah BAWD-hee-t'l.

1091. A bathing suit.

אַ באָדקאָסטיום·

ah BAWD-kawst-yoom.

1092. A blouse.

אַ בלוזע·

ah BLOO-zeh.

1093. A brassiere.

אַ סטאַניק·

ah STAH-nik.

1094. A coat.

אַ מאַנטל·

ah MAHN-t'l.

1095. A collar.

אַ קאָלנער·

ah KAWL-nehr.

1096. A collar pin.

אַ קאָלנער־שפּילקע·

ah KAWL-nehr-shpeel-keh.

1097. A pair of cuff links.

אַ פֿאָר שפֿאַנקעס·

ah pawr SHPAWN-kes.

1098. Diapers.

וװינדעלעך׃

VIN-deh-lekh.

1099. A dress.

א קלײד׃

ah KLAYD.

1100. A pair of garters.

א פאר זאָקנבענדלעך׃

ah pawr ZAW-k'n-bend-lekh.

1101. A girdle.

א קאָרסעט׃

ah kawr-SET.

1102. A pair of gloves.

א פאר הענטשקעס׃

ah pawr HENCH-kes

1103. Handkerchiefs.

נאָזטיכלעך׃

NAWZ-teckh-lekh.

1104. A hat.

א הוט׃

ah HOOT.

1105. A jacket.

א זשאקעט׃

ah zhah-KET.

1106. A necktie.

א שניפס׃

ah SHNIPS.

1107. A nightgown.

א נאכטהעמד׃

ah NAHKHT-hemd.

1108. An overcoat.

אן אײבערמאַנטל׃

ahn AY-behr-mahn-t'l.

1109. A pair of pajamas.

א פיזשאַמע׃

ah pee-ZHAH-meh.

1110. A pair of panties.

א פּאָר הייזעלעך·

ah pawr HAYZ-lekh.

1111. A petticoat.

אן אונטערקלייד·

ahn OON-tehr-klayd.

1112. A raincoat.

א רעגן־מאַנטל·

ah REH-g'n-mahn-t'l.

1113. A robe.

א כאַלאַט·

ah khah-LAHT.

1114. A pair of sandals.

א פּאָר סאַנדאַלן·

ah pawr sahn-DAH-l'n.

1115. A scarf.

א שאַרפֿל·

ah SHAHR-f'l.

1116. A shirt.

א העמד·

ah HEMD.

1117. A pair of shoes.

א פּאָר שיך·

ah pawr SHEEKH.

1118. A pair of shorts.

א פּאָר אונטערהויזן·

ah pawr OON-tehr-hoy-z'n.

1119. A skirt.

א קליידל·

ah KLAY-d'l.

1120. A pair of slacks.

א פּאָר הויזן·

ah pawr HOY-z'n.

1121. A slip.

אן אונטערקליידל·

ahn OON-tehr-klay-d'l.

1122. A pair of slippers.

אַ פּאָר שטעקשיך•

ah pawr SHTEK-sheekh.

1123. Socks.

סקאַרפּעטן•

skahr-PEH-t'n.

1124. A sport shirt.

אַ ספּאָרטהעמד•

ah SPORT-hemd.

1125. A pair of (nylon) stockings.

אַ פּאָר (נײלאָנענע) זאָקן•

ah pawr (NI-law-neh-neh) ZAW-k'n.

1126. A suit.

אַ קאָסטיום•

ah kawst-YOOM.

1127. A pair of suspenders.

אַ פּאָר שלייקעס•

ah pawr SHLAY-kess.

1128. A sweater.

אַ סוועטער•

ah SVEH-tehr.

1129. An undershirt.

אַן אונטערהעמד•

ahn OON-tehr-hemd.

1130. Underwear.

אונטערוועש•

OON-tehr-vesh.

1131. A vest.

אַ וועסטל•

ah VES-t'l.

MEASUREMENTS

1132. What is the size?

וועלכע גרייס איז עס?

VEL-kheh GRAYS iz es?

1133. What is the length (width)?

ווי‌פֿ‌ל האַלט די לענג (ברייט)?

VEE-f'l HAHLT dee LENGG (BRAYT)?

1134. Large.	**1135. Small.**	**1136. Medium.**
גרויס.	קליין.	מיטל.
groyss.	*klayn.*	*MIT'l.*

1137. Larger.	**1138. Smaller.**
גרעסער.	קלענער.
GREH-sehr.	*KLEH-nehr.*

1139. Longer.	**1140. Shorter.**
לענגער.	קירצער.
LEN-gehr.	*KEER-tsehr.*

1141. Wider.	**1142. Narrower.**
ברייטער.	שמעלער.
BRAY-tehr.	*SHMEH-lehr.*

1143. Heavier.	**1144. Thinner.**
שווערער.	דינער.
SHVEH-rehr.	*DIN-nehr.*

1145. High.	**1146. Low.**
הויך.	נידעריק.
hoykh.	*NID-eh-rik.*

COLORS

1147. I want a lighter (darker) shade.

איך וויל אַ העלערע (טונקעלערע) שאַטירונג.

eekh VIL ah HEH-leh-reh (TOON-keh-leh-reh) shah-TEE-roongg.

1148. Light.

העל.

hel.

1149. Dark.
טונקל·
TOON-k'l.

1150. Black.
שוואַרץ·
shvahrts.

1151. Blue.
בלוי·
bloy.

1152. Brown.
ברוין·
broyn.

1153. Cream.
קרעם·
krem.

1154. Gray.
גרוי·
groy.

1155. Green.
גרין·
green.

1156. Orange.
אָראַנזש·
aw-RAHNZH.

1157. Pink.
ראָזע·
RAW-zeh.

1158. Purple.
לילאַ·
LEE-lah.

1159. Red.

רויט.

royt.

1160. White.

ווײַס.

vīs.

1161. Yellow.

געל.

gel.

BOOKSTORE AND STATIONER'S

1162. Where is there a bookshop?

וואו איז פֿאַראַן אַ ביכערקראָם?

VOO eez fah-RAHN ah BEE-khehr-krawm?

1163. Can you recommend a book about ——?

צי קענט איר רעקאָמענדירן אַ בוך וועגן ——?

tsee KENT eer reh-kaw-men-DEE-r'n ah BOOKH veh-g'n ——?

1164. I want a map of ——.

איך דאַרף אַ קאַרטע פֿון ——.

eekh DAHRF ah KAHR-teh foon ——.

1165. A stationer's.

אַ פּאַפּירקראָם.

ah pah-PEER-krawm.

1166. A newsdealer.

אַ צײַטונג־פֿאַרקױפֿער.

ah TSI-toongg-fahr-koy-fehr.

1167. Artist's materials.

קינסטלער־מאַטעריאַלן.

KINST-lehr-mah-tehr-yah-l'n.

1168. A book.
אַ בוך.
ah BOOKH.

1169. Blotter.
לעשפּאַפּיר.
LESH-pah-peer.

1170. Carbon paper.
קאַלקע.
KAHL-keh.

1171. A dictionary.
אַ ווערטערבוך.
ah VEHR-tehr-bookh.

1172. (Airmail) envelopes.
(לופֿטפּאָסט־) קאַנווערטן.
(LOOFT-pawst) kawn-VEHR-t'n.

1173. An eraser.
אַ מעקער.
ah MEH-kehr.

1174. A fountain pen.
אַן אייביקע פֿעדער.
ahn AY-bee-keh FEH-dehr.

1175. Some greeting cards.
באַגריס־קאַרטלעך.
bah-GREES-kahrt-lekh.

1176. Ink.
טינט.
tint.

1177. Magazines.
זשורנאַלן.
zhoor-NAH-l'n.

1178. Newspapers.
צייטונגען־
TSI-toon-gen.

1179. A pencil.
א בלייער־
ah BLI-ehr.

1180. Playing cards.
קָארטן־
KOR-t'n.

1181. Postcards.
פָּאסטקַארטעלעך־
PAWST-kahrt-lekh.

1182. Scotch tape.
קלעפּ־צעלאָפָאַן־
KLEP-tseh-law-fahn.

1183. String.
שטריק־
shtrik.

1184. Tissue paper.
זײדפּאַפּיר־
ZID-pah-peer.

1185. A typewriter ribbon.
א שרײבמאַשין־באַנד־
ah SHRIB-mah-sheen-bahnd.

1186. Wrapping paper.
פּאַקפּאַפּיר־
PAHK-pah-peer.

1187. Writing paper.
שרײבפּאַפּיר־
SHRIB-pah-peer.

CIGAR STORE

1188. Where is the nearest cigar store?

װאו איז די נאָענטסטע ציגאַרן־קראָם?

VOO iz dee NAW-ent-steh tsee-GAH-r'n-krawm?

1189. Give me some cigars.

גיט מיר ציגאַרן∙

GIT meer tsee-GAH-r'n.

1190. A pack of (American) cigarettes, please.

אַ פּעקל (אַמעריקאַנער) פּאַפּיראָסן, זײַט אַזױ
גוט∙

ah PEH-k'l (ah-meh-ree-KAH-nehr) pah-pee-RAW-s'n, ZIT ah-zoy GOOT.

1191. Please show me some cigarette cases.

זײַט אַזױ גוט, װײַזט מיר פּאַפּיראָסן־האַלטערס∙

ZIT ah-zoy GOOT, VIST meer pah-pee-RAW-s'n-hahl-tehrs.

1192. I need a lighter.

איך דאַרף אָן אָנצינדער∙

eekh DAHRF ahn AWN-tseen-dehr.

1193. May I have a match (a light), please?

גיט מיר אַ שװעבעלע (פֿײַער), זײַט אַזױ גוט∙

*GIT meer ah SHVEH-beh-leh (FI-ehr), ZIT ah-zoy
GOOT.*

1194. Flint.

פֿײַערשטײן∙

FI-ehr-shtayn.

1195. Lighter fluid.

אָנצינדער־פֿליסיקײט∙

AWN-tsin-dehr-flee-see-kit.

1196. Matches.

שוועבעלעך׃

SHVEH-beh-lekh.

1197. A pipe.

א ליולקע׃

ah LYOOL-keh.

1198. Pipe tobacco.

ליולקע־טאַבאַק׃

LYOOL-keh-tah-bahk.

1199. A pouch.

א טאַבאַקזעקל׃

ah TAH-bahk-zeh-k'l.

PHOTOGRAPHY

1200. I want a roll of (color) film.

איך וויל א שפולקע (קאָלירטן) פֿילם׃

eekh VIL ah SHPOOL-keh (kaw-LEER-t'n) FILM.

1201. The size is ——.

די מאָס איז ——׃

dee MAWS iz ——.

1202. For this camera.

פֿאַר דעם אַפּאַראַט׃

fahr DEM ah-pah-RAHT.

1203. Movie film.

קינאָ־פֿילם׃

KEE-naw-film.

1204. Flashbulbs.

בליצלאָמפּן׃

BLITS-lawm-p'n.

1205. What is the charge for developing a roll?

וויפֿל קאָסט אַנטוויקלען א שפולקע?

VEE-f'l COST ahnt-VIK-len ah SHPOOL-keh?

1206. One print of each.

איין קאָפּיע פֿון יעדן׃

AYN KAWP-yeh foon YEH-d'n.

1207. An enlargement.

א פֿאַרגרעסערונג׃

ah fahr-GREH-seh-roongg.

1208. When will they be ready?

ווען וועלן זיי פֿאַרטיק ווערן?

VEN veh-l'n zay FAHR-tik veh-r'n?

1209. The camera is out of order.

דער אַפּאַראַט איז קאַליע.

dehr ah-pah-RAHT iz KAHL-yeh.

1210. Do you rent cameras?

צי פֿאַרדינגט איר אַפּאַראַטן?

tsee fahr-DINGT eer ah-pah-RAH-t'n?

1211. Would you mind letting me take your picture?

צי וועט עס אײַך שטערן אויב איך נעם פֿון
אײַך אַ בילד?

tsee vet es ikh SHTEH-r'n oyb eekh NEM foon ikh ah BILD?

DRUG STORE

1212. Where is there a drug store where they understand English?

וואו איז דאָ אַן אַפּטייקקראָם וואו מען פֿאַר־
שטייט ענגליש?

VOO iz daw ahn ahp-TAYK-krawm voo men fahr-SHTAYT ENGG-lish?

1213. Can you fill this prescription?

צי קענט איר מיר צוגרייטן דעם רעצעפט?

tsee KENT eer meer TSOO-gray-t'n dem reh-TSEPT?

1214. How long will it take?

ווי לאַנג וועט עס געדויערן?

VEE LAHNGG vet es geh-DOY-eh-r'n?

1215. Can you deliver it to this address?

צי קענט איר עס צושטעלן אויף דעם אַדרעס?

tsee KENT eer es TSOO-shteh-l'n oyf DEM AHD-res?

1216. I want adhesive tape.

איך דַארף אַ פּלַאסטער׃

eekh DAHRF ah PLAHS-tehr.

1217. The alcohol.

דער אַלקאָהאָל׃

dehr AHL-kaw-hawl.

1218. An antiseptic.

אַן אַנטיסעפּטיק׃

ahn ahn-tee-SEP-tik.

1219. The aspirin.

די אַספּירין׃

dee ahs-pee-REEN.

1220. The bandages.

די באַנדאַזשן׃

dee bahn-DAH-zh'n.

1221. The bicarbonate of soda.

דער סאָדע־פּראַשיק׃

dehr SAW-deh-praw-shik.

1222. The boric acid.

דאָס באָרזיערס׃

daws BAWR-zĭ-ehrs.

1223. The epsom salts.

די ביטערואַלץ׃

dee BIT-ehr-zahlts.

1224. The eye cup.

דאָס גלעזל צום שוועכקען דאָס אויג׃

daws GLEH-z'l tsoom SHVEN-ken daws OYG.

1225. The face tissues.

די פּאַפּירטיכלעך צום פּנים׃

dee pah-PEER-teekh-lekh tsoom PAW-nim.

1226. The gargle.

דאָס שוועכקעכץ צום האַלדז׃

daws SHVENK-ekhts tsoom HAHLDZ.

1227. The gauze.

די מערלע·

dee MEHR-leh.

1228. The hot water bottle.

די וואֿרעמפֿלאַש·

dee VAH-rem-flahsh.

1229. The ice bag.

דער אײזזאַק·

dehr IZ-zahk.

1230. The insect bite lotion.

דאָס שמירעכץ קעגן אינסעקטן־ביסן·

daws SHMEE-rekhts keh-g'n in-SEK-t'n-bis'n.

1231. The insect repellent.

דער אינסעקטן־אָפּטרײבער·

dehr in-SEK-t'n-awp-tri-behr.

1232. The iodine.

די יאָד·

dee YAWD.

1233. The hair (tooth) brush.

די האָר־ (צאָן־) באַרשט·

dee HAWR- (TSAWN-) bahrsht.

1234. The castor oil.

דער ריצנאײל·

dehr RIT-s'n-ayl.

1235. The cold cream.

דער הויטקרעם·

dehr HOYT-krem.

1236. The comb.

דער קאַם·

dehr KAHM.

1237. The corn pads.

די פּלאַסטערס פֿאַר הינעראויגן·

dee PLAHS-tehrs fahr HEE-nehr-oy-g'n.

1239. The cotton.

די וואַטע·

dee VAH-teh.

1239. The depilatory.

דאָס מיטל קעגן האָר.

daws MIT'l keh-g'n HAWR.

1240. The deodorant.

דאָס מיטל קעגן ריחות.

daws MIT'l keh-g'n RAY-khes.

1241. The ear stoppers.

די אויער־קאָרקעס.

dee OY-ehr-kor-kes.

1242. The laxative (mild).

די אָפֿפֿירונג (מילדע).

dee AWP-fee-roongg (MEEL-deh).

1243. The lipstick.

דער ליפנשטיפֿט.

dehr LIP'n-shtift.

1244. The medicine dropper.

די פּיפּעטקע.

dee pee-PET-keh.

1245. The mouthwash.

דאָס שווענקעכץ פֿאַרן מויל.

daws SHVENK-ekhts fah-r'n MOYL.

1246. The nail file.

די נעגלפֿײַל.

dee NEH-g'l-fil.

1247. The nail polish.

דער נעגל־לאַקיר.

dehr NEH-g'l-lah-keer.

1248. The peroxide.

דער סופּעראָקסיד.

dehr SOO-pehr-awk-SEED.

1249. The powder.

דער פּודער.

dehr POO-dehr.

1250. The razor.

דער גאַלער.

dehr GAW-lehr.

1251. The razor blades.

די גאַלמעסערלעך.

dee GAWL-meh-sehr-lekh.

1252. The rouge.

די שמינקע.

dee SHMIN-keh.

1253. The sanitary napkins.

די דאַמען־באַנדאַזשן.

dee DAH-men-bahn-dah-zh'n.

1254. The sedative.

דאָס באַרויק־מיטל.

daws bah-ROO-eek-mit'l.

1255. The shampoo (liquid, cream).

דער שאַמפּו (די פֿליסיקייט, דער קרעם).

dehr shahm-POO (dee FLEE-see-kit, dehr KREM).

1256. The shaving lotion.

דאָס גאַלשמירעכץ.

daws GAWL-shmee-rekhts.

1257. The shaving cream (brushless).

דער גאַלקרעם (אָן אַ פּענדזל).

dehr GAWL-krem (AWN ah PEN-dz'l).

1258. The bar of soap.

דאָס שטיק זייף.

daws SHTIK ZAYF.

1259. The box of soap flakes.

דאָס קעסטל זייף־שנייעלעך.

daws KES-t'l ZAYF-shnay-eh-lekh.

1260. The sunburn ointment.

די זונברען־זאַלב.

dee ZOON-bren-zahlb.

1261. The smelling salts.

די חלשות־טראָפּנס.

dee khah-LAW-shes-traw-p'ns.

1262. The suntan oil.

דער זונברען־אײל.

dehr ZOON-bren-ayl.

1263. The thermometer.

דער טערמאָמעטער.

dehr tehr-maw-MEH-tehr.

1264. The toilet tissue.

דאָס קלאָזעט־פּאַפּיר.

daws klaw-ZET-pah-peer.

1265. The toothpaste.

די צאָנפּאַסטע.

dee TSAWN-pahs-teh.

1266. The toothpowder.

דער צאָנפּראָשיק.

dehr TSAWN-praw-shik.

BARBER SHOP AND BEAUTY PARLOR

1267. Where is there a good barber?

וואו איז דאָ אַ גוטער שערער?

VOO iz daw ah GOO-tehr SHEH-rehr?

1268. I want a haircut (a shave).

איך וויל זיך אָפּשערן (אָפּגאָלן).

eekh VIL zikh AWP-sheh-r'n (AWP-gaw-l'n).

1269. Not too short.

ניט צו קורץ.

NEET TSOO KOORTS.

1270. Do not cut any off the top.

שערט ניט פֿון אויבן.

SHEHRT nit foon OY-b'n.

1271. Do not put on oil.

שמירט ניט אָן קיין פֿעטס•

SHMEERT nit AWN kayn FETS.

1272. I part my hair on the (other) side.

איך מאַך זיך אַ שׁרונט אויף דער (אַנדערער) זײַט•

eekh MAHKH zikh ah SHROONT oyf dehr (AHN-deh-rer) ZIT.

1273. In the middle.

אין מיטן•

in MIT'n.

1274. The water is too hot (cold).

דאָס וואַסער איז צו הייס (קאַלט)•

daws VAH-sehr iz TSOO HAYS (KAHLT).

1275. I want my shoes shined.

איך וויל לאָזן אָפּפוצן די שיך•

eekh VIL law-z'n AWP-poo-ts'n dee SHEEKH.

1276. Can I make an appointment for ——?

צי קען איך מאַכן אַ באַשטעלונג אויף ——?

tsee KEN eekh MAH-kh'n ah bah-SHTEH-loongg oyf ——?

1277. I should like a new hair style.

איך וויל אַ נײַע פֿריזור•

eekh VIL ah NI-eh free-ZOOR.

1278. I want to tint (to bleach) my hair.

איך וויל אָפּפֿאַרבן (אויסבלאַנקירן) די האָר•

eekh VIL AWP-fahr-b'n (OYS-blahn-kee-r'n) dee HAWR.

1279. May I see the color samples?

צי קען איך זען די קאָליר־מוסטערן?

tsee KEN eekh ZEN dee kaw-LEER-moos-teh-r'n?

1280. A finger wave.

א פינגער־אָנדולירונג·

ah FEEN-gehr-awn-doo-lee-roongg.

1281. A permanent wave.

א פּערמאַנענטע אָנדולירונג·

ah pehr-mah-NEN-teh awn-doo-LEE-roongg.

1282. A shampoo.

א שאַמפּוירונג·

ah shahm-poo-EE-roongg.

1283. A facial.

א באַהאַנדלונג פֿון פּנים·

ah bah-HAHND-loongg foon PAW-nim.

1284. A manicure.   **1285. A massage.**

א מאַניקיר·   א מאַסאַזש·

ah mah-nee-KEER.   *ah mah-SAHZH.*

1286. Where can I see a chiropodist?

וואו איז פֿאַראַן א פֿוסדאַקטערי?

VOO iz fah-RAHN ah FOOS-dawk-tehr?

1287. A Turkish bath.

א שוויצבאַד·

ah SHVITS-bawd.

LAUNDRY AND DRY CLEANING

1288. Where is the laundry (the dry cleaner)?

וואו איז די וועשערי (דער כעמישער רייניקער)?

VOO iz dee veh-sheh-RI (dehr KHEH-mee-shehr RAY-nee-kehr)?

1289. I want to have this shirt washed (mended).

איך וויל לאָזן אויסוואַשן (פֿאַרריכטן) דאָס העמד·

eekh VIL law-z'n OYS-vah-sh'n (fahr-REEKH-t'n) daws HEMD.

1290. Can you have this suit cleaned (pressed)?

צי קענט איר לאָזן אויסריינינן (אויספרעסן)
דעם קאָסטיום?

tsee KENT eer law-z'n OYS-ray-nee-k'n (OYS-preh-s'n) dem kawst-YOOM?

1291. Do not wash in hot water.

וואַשט עס ניט אין הייס וואַסער·

VAHSHT es nit in HAYS VAH-sehr.

1292. Use lukewarm water.

ניצט לעבלעך וואַסער·

NITST LEB-lekh VAH-sehr.

1293. Be very careful.

זײַט זייער אָפּגעהיט·

ZIT ZAY-ehr AWP-geh-heet.

1294. Remove this stain.

נעמט אַרויס דעם פֿלעק·

NEMT ah-ROYS dem FLEK.

1295. Do not dry this in the sun.

טריקנט עס ניט אויף דער זון·

TRIK-n't es nit oyf der ZOON.

1296. (Do not) starch the collars.

טוט (ניט) אַרײַן קראַכמאַל אין די קאָלנערס·

TOOT (nit) ah-RIN KRAWKH-mahl in dee KAWL- nehrs.

1297. When can I have this back?

ווען קען איך עס קריגן צוריק?

VEN KEN eekh es KRIG'n tsoo-RIK?

1298. The belt is missing.

עס פֿעלט דער גאַרטל·

es FEHLT dehr GAHR-t'l.

ILLNESS

1299. I wish to see a doctor (a specialist).

איך וויל זיך זען מיט אַ דאָקטער (אַ ספּעציאַ־
ליסט)•

eekh VIL zikh ZEN mit ah DAWK-tehr (ah spets-yah-LIST).

1300. An American doctor.

אַן אַמעריקאַנער דאָקטער•

ahn ah-meh-ree-KAH-nehr DAWK-tehr.

1301. I do not sleep well.

איך שלאָף ניט גוט•

eekh SHLAWF nit GOOT.

1302. My foot hurts.

דער פֿוס טוט מיר וויי•

dehr FOOS toot meer VAY.

1303. My head aches.

דער קאָפּ טוט מיר וויי•

dehr KAWP toot meer VAY.

1304. I have a virus.

איך האָב אַ ווירוס•

eekh HAWB ah VEE-roos.

1305. Can you give me something to relieve my allergy?

צי קענט איר מיר עפּעס געבן צו פֿאַרלײַכטערן
די אַלערגיע?

tsee KENT eer meer eh-pes GEH-b'n tsoo fahr-LIKH-teh-r'n dee ah-LERG-yeh?

1306. Appendicitis.

אַפּענדיציט•

ah-pen-dee-TSEET.

1307. Biliousness.
גאַלקראַנקייט·
GAHL-krahn-kĭt.

1308. A bite.
אַ ביס·
ah BIS.

1309. An insect bite.
אַן אינסעקטן־ביס·
ahn in-SEK-t'n-bis.

1310. A blister.
אַ פּענכער·
ah PEN-khehr.

1311. A boil.
אַ בלאָטער·
ah BLAW-tehr.

1312. A burn.
אַ ברי·
ah BREE.

1313. Chills.
ציטערן·
TSIT-eh-r'n.

1314. A cold.
אַ פאַרקילונג·
ah fahr-KEE-loongg.

1315. Constipation.
פאַרשטאָפּונג·
fahr-SHTAW-poongg.

1316. A cough.
אַ הוסט·
ah HOOST.

1317. A cramp.
אַ קראַמף·
ah KRAHMF.

1318. Diarrhoea.
שילשול·
SHIL- sh'l.

1319. Dysentery.
דיסענטעריע·
dee-sen-TEHR-yeh.

1320. An earache.
אַן אויער־ווייטיק·
ahn OY-ehr-vay-tik.

1321. A fever.
היץ·
hits.

1322. Hay fever.
הייפֿיבער·
HAY-fee-behr.

1323. Hoarseness.
הייזעריקייט·
HAY-zeh-ree-kīt.

1324. Indigestion.
בויכווייטיק·
BOYKH-vay-tik.

1325. Nausea.
ניטגוטקייט·
nit-GOOT-kīt.

1326. Pneumonia.
לונגען־אָנצינדונג·
LOON-gen-awn-tseen-doongg.

1327. A sore throat.

האלדזוווייטיק.

HAHLD Ẕ-vay-tik.

1328. Chafed.

אָנגעריבן.

AWN-geh-ree-b'n.

1329. A sprain.

אן אויסלינקונג.

ahn OYS-leen-koongg.

1330. Sun burn.

אן אָפּברען פֿון דער זון.

ahn AWP-bren foon dehr ẔOON.

1331. A sun stroke.

אַ זונשלאַק.

ah ẔOON-shlahk.

1332. Typhoid fever.

פֿלעקטיפֿוס.

FLEK-tee-foos.

1333. To vomit.

אויסברעכן.

OYS-breh-kh'n.

1334. What am I to do?

וואָס דאַרף איך טאָן?

VAWS dahrf eekh TAWN?

1335. Must I stay in bed?

צי מוז איך ליגן אין בעט?

tsee MOO Ẕ eekh LIG'n in BET?

1336. Do I have to go to a hospital?

צי דאַרף איך גיין אַ שפּיטאָל?

tsee DAHRF eekh GAYN in ah shpee-TAWL?

1337. May I get up?

צי מעג איך אויפֿשטיין?

tsee MEG eekh OYF-shtayn?

1338. I feel better.

מיר איז בעסער.

meer iz BEH-sehr.

1339. When do you think I'll be better?

ווען רעכנט איר וועט מיר ווערן בעסער?

VEN REH-kh'nt eer vet meer VEH-r'n BEH-sehr?

1340. Can I travel on Monday?

צי קען איך פֿאָרן מאָנטיק?

tsee KEN eekh FAW-r'n MAWN-tik?

1341. When will you come again?

ווען וועט איר ווידער קומען?

VEN vet eer VID-ehr KOO-men?

1342. Please write out a medical bill.

זײַט אַזוי גוט, שרײַבט מיר אָן אַ מעדיצינישע
רעכענונג.

*ZIT ah-zoy GOOT, SHRIPT meer AWN ah meh-
dee-TSEE-nee-sheh REH-kheh-noongg.*

1343. A drop.

אַ טראָפּן.

ah TRAW-p'n.

1344. A teaspoonful.

אַ לעפֿעלע.

ah LEH-feh-leh.

1345. The medicine.

די מעדיצין.

dee meh-dee-TSEEN.

1346. Twice a day.

צוויי מאָל אַ טאָג.

*TSVAY mawl ah
TAWG.*

1347. Hot water.

הייס וואַסער.

HAYS VAH-sehr.

1348. A pill.

א פּיל·

ah PIL.

1349. A prescription.

א רעצעפּט·

ah reh-TSEPT.

1350. Every hour.

אלע שעה·

AH-leh SHAW.

1351. Before (after) meals.

פֿאַרן (נאָכן) עסן

*FAH-r'n (NAW-kh'n)
EH-s'n*

1352. On going to bed.

בײם גײן שלאָפֿן·

bĭm GAYN SHLAW-f'n.

1353. On getting up.

בײם אויפֿשטײן·

bĭm OYF-shtayn.

1354. X-rays.

רענטגען־שטראַלן·

RENT-gen-shtrah-l'n.

See also DRUG STORE, page 127.

ACCIDENTS

1355. There has been an accident.

עס האָט געטראָפֿן אַן אומגליק·

es hawt geh-TRAW-f'n ahn OOM-glik.

1356. Get a doctor (a nurse).

ברענגט אַ דאָקטער (אַ קראַנקן־שוועסטער)·

*BRENGT ah DAWK-tehr (ah KRAHN-k'n-
shves-tehr).*

1357. Send for an ambulance.

שיקט נאָך אַן אמבולאַנס·

SHIKT nawkh ahn ahm-boo-LAHNS.

1358. Please bring blankets.

זײט אַזוי גוט· ברענגט קאָלדרעס·

ZIT ah-zoy GOOT, BRENGT KAWL-dres.

1359. A stretcher.

אַ טראַגבעטל.

ah TRAWG-beh-t'l.

1360. Water.

װאַסער.

VAH-sehr.

1361. He is (seriously) injured.

ער איז (ערנצט) פֿאַרװאונדט.

ehr iz (EH-r'ntst) fahr-VOONT.

1362. Help me carry him.

העלפֿט מיר אים טראָגן.

HELFT meer eem TRAW-g'n.

1363. He was knocked down.

מען האָט אים אַנידערגעשלײַדערט.

men hawt eem ah-NID-ehr-geh-shlī-dehrt.

1364. She has fallen (has fainted).

זי איז געפֿאַלן (האָט געחלשט).

zee iz geh-FAH-l'n (hawt geh-KHAH-lesht).

1365. I feel weak.

איך פֿיל זיך שװאַך.

eekh FEEL zikh SHVAHKH.

1366. He has a fracture (a bruise, a cut).

ער האָט אַ צעבראָכענעם בײן (אַ סיניאַק, אַ שניט).

ehr hawt ah tseh-BRAW-kheh-nem BAYN (ah sin-YAHK, ah SHNIT).

1367. He has burned (cut) his hand.

ער האָט זיך פֿאַרברענט (צעשניטן) די האַנט.

ehr hawt zikh fahr-BRENT (tseh-SHNIT'n) dee HAHNT.

1368. It is bleeding.

עס גייט בלוט.

es GAYT BLOOT.

1369. It is swollen.

עס איז געשוואָלן•

es iz geh-SHVAW-l'n.

1370. Can you dress this?

צי קענט איר עס פֿאַרבאַנדאַזשירן?

tsee KENT eer es fahr-bahn-dah-ZHEE-r'n?

1371. Have you any bandages or splints?

צי האָט איר באַנדאַזשן אָדער ברעטלעך?

tsee HAWT eer bahn-DAH-zh'n aw-dehr BRET-lekh?

1372. I need something for a tourniquet.

איך דאַרף עפּעס אויף אַ טורניקעט•

eekh DAHRF eh-pes oyf ah toor-nee-KET.

1373. Are you all right?

צי פֿעלט אײך עפּעס?

tsee FELT ikh EH-pes?

1374. It hurts here.

עס טוט וויי דאָ•

es toot VAY DAW.

1375. I want to sit down a moment.

איך וויל זיך אַ ווײלע צוזעצן•

eekh VIL zikh ah VI-leh TSOO-zeh-ts'n.

1376. I cannot move my ——.

איך קען ניט רירן מײַן ——•

eekh KEN nit REE-r'n min ——.

1377. I have hurt my ——.

איך האָב זיך וויי געטאָן מײַן ——•

eekh hawb zikh VAY geh-tawn min ——.

See PARTS OF THE BODY, page 144.

1378. Please notify my husband (my wife).

זײט אַזױ גוט, גיט צו װיסן מײַן מאַן (מײַן פֿרױ)·

ZIT ah-zoy GOOT, GIT tsoo VIS'n min MAHN
(min FROY).

1379. Here is my identification (my card).

אָט איז מײַן לעגיטימאַציע (מײַן װיזיט־קאַרטל)·

AWT iz min leh-gee-tee-MAHTS-yeh (min vee-
ZIT-kahr-t'l).

1380. I have broken (lost) my eye glasses.

איך האָב צעבראָכן (פֿאַרלױרן) די ברילן·

eekh hawb tseh-BRAW-kh'n (fahr-LOY-r'n) dee
BRIL'n.

1381. Where can I find an optometrist?

װאו קען איך געפֿינען אַן אָפּטיקער?

VOO ken eekh geh-FIN-en ahn AWP-tee-kehr?

1382. Who can fix this hearing aid?

װער קען פֿאַרריכטן דעם הער־אַפּאַראַט?

VEHR ken fahr-REEKH-t'n DEM HEHR-ah-pah-
raht?

PARTS OF THE BODY

1383. The ankle.

דאָס קנעכל·

daws KNEH-kh'l.

1384. The appendix.

די בלינדע קישקע·

dee BLIN-deh KISH-keh.

1385. The arm.

דער אָרעם·

dehr AW-rem.

1386. The back.

די פּלייצע·

dee PLAY-tseh.

1387. The blood.
דאָס בלוט׳
daws BLOOT.

1388. The bone.
דער ביין׳
dehr BAYN.

1389. The breast.
די ברוסט׳
dee BROOST.

1390. The cheek.
די באַק׳
dee BAHK.

1391. The chest.
די ברוסט׳
dee BROOST.

1392. The chin.
די קין׳
dee KIN.

1393. The collar bone.
דער קאָלנערביין׳
dehr KAWL-nehr-bayn.

1394. The ear.
דער אויער׳
dehr OY-ehr.

1395. The elbow.
דער עלנבויגן׳
dehr EH-l'n-boy-g'n.

1396. The eye.
דאָס אויג׳
daws OYG.

1397. The eyebrows.
די ברעמען׳
dee BREH-men.

1398. The eyelashes.
די וויִעס׳
dee VEE-es.

1399. The eyelid.

דאָס אויג־לעדל·

daws OY-g'n-leh-d'l

1400. The face.

דאָס פּנים·

daws PAW-nim.

1401. The finger.

דער פֿינגער·

dehr FIN-gehr.

1402. The foot.

דער פֿוס·

dehr FOOS.

1403. The forehead.

דער שטערן·

dehr SHTEH-r'n.

1404. The hair.

די האָר·

dee HAWR.

1405. The hand.

די האַנט·

dee HAHNT.

1406. The head.

דער קאָפּ·

dehr KAWP.

1407. The heart.

דאָס האַרץ·

daws HAHRTS.

1408. The heel.

די פּיאַטע·

dee PYAH-teh.

1409. The hip.

די לענד·

dee LEND.

1410. The intestines.

די אינגעווייד·

dee IN-geh-vayd.

1411. The jaw.
דער קינביין·
dehr KIN-bayn.

1412. The joint.
דאָס געלענק·
daws geh-LENK.

1413. The kidney.
די ניר·
dee NEER.

1414. The knee.
דער קני·
dee K'NEE.

1415. The leg.
דער פוס·
dehr FOOS.

1416. The lip.
די ליפ·
dee LIP.

1417. The liver.
די לעבער·
dee LEH-behr.

1418. The lung.
די לונג·
dee LOONGG.

1419. The mouth.
דאָס מויל·
daws MOYL.

1420. The muscle.
דער מוסקל·
dehr MOOS-k'l.

1421. The nail.
דער נאָגל·
dehr NAW-g'l.

1422. The neck.
דער נאָקן·
dehr NAH-k'n.

1423. The nerve.

דער נערװ־

dehr NEHRV.

1424. The nose.

די נאָז־

dee NAWZ.

1425. The rib.

די ריפ־

dee RIP.

1426. The shoulder.

דער אַקסל־

dehr AHK-s'l.

1427. The right (left) side.

די רעכטע (לינקע) זײט־

dee REKH-teh (LIN-keh) ZIT.

1428. The skin.

די הױט־

dee HOYT.

1429. The skull.

דער שאַרבן־

dehr SHAHR-b'n.

1430. The spine.

דער רוקנבײן־

dehr ROO-k'n-bayn.

1431. The stomach.

דער מאָגן־

dehr MAW-g'n.

1432. The thigh.

די דיך־

dee DEEKH.

1433. The throat.

דער האַלדז־

dehr HAHLDZ.

1434. The thumb.

דער גראָבער פֿינגער־

dehr GRAW-behr FIN-gehr.

1435. The toe.

דער פֿינגער פֿון פֿוס·

dehr FIN-gehr foon FOOS.

1436. The tongue.

די צונג·

dee TSOONGG.

1437. The tonsils.

די מאַנדלען·

dee MAHND-len.

1438. The wrist.

דאָס האַנטגעלענק·

daws HAHNT-geh-lenk.

DENTIST

1439. Do you know a good dentist?

צי קענט איר אַ גוטן צאָנדאָקטער?

tsee KENT eer ah GOO-t'n TSAWN-dawk-tehr?

1440. This tooth hurts.

דער צאָן טוט מיר וויי·

DEHR TSAWN toot meer VAY.

1441. Can you fix it temporarily?

צי קענט איר אים באַהאַנדלען אויף דער ווײַל?

tsee KENT eer eem bah-HAHND-len oyf dehr VIL?

1442. I have lost a filling.

איך האָב פֿאַרלוירן אַ פּלאָמבע·

eekh hawb fahr-LOY-r'n ah PLAWM-beh.

1443. I have an abscess.

איך האָב אַ געשוויר·

eekh HAWB ah geh-SHVEER.

1444. I have broken a tooth.

איך האָב צעבראָכן אַ צאָן·

eekh hawb tseh-BRAW-kh'n ah TSAWN.

1445. I (do not) want it extracted.

איך וויל אים (ניט) אַרויסרײַסן•

eekh VIL eem (nit) ah-ROYS-rī-s'n.

1446. Can you save it?

צי קענט איר אים אָפּראַטעווען?

tsee KENT eer eem AWP-rah-teh-ven?

1447. You are hurting me.

איר טוט מיר ווײ•

eer TOOT meer VAY.

1448. Can you repair this denture (this bridge)?

צי קענט איר פֿאַרריכטן די קינסטלעכע ציין
(דאָס צאָנבריקל)?

tsee KENT eer fahr-REEKH-t'n dee KINST-leh-kheh TSAYN (daws TSAWN-brik'l)?

1449. Local anesthetic.

לאָקאַלע אַנעסטעטיע•

law-KAH-leh ah-nes-TEHZ-yeh.

1450. The gums.

די יאָסלעס•

dee YAHS-les.

1451. The nerve.

דער נערוו•

dehr NEHRV.

POST OFFICE

1452. Where is the post office?

וואו איז די פּאָסט?

VOO eez dee PAWST?

1453. To which window do I go?

צו וועלכן פֿענצטער זאָל איך גיין?

tsoo VEL-kh'n FENTS-tehr zawl eekh GAYN?

1454. Post card.

פּאָסטקאַרטל•

PAWST-kahr-t'l.

1455. Letter.

בריוו•

breev.

1456. By airmail.

מיט לופטפּאָסט·

mit LOOFT-pawst.

1457. Parcel post.

פּעקלפּאָסט·

PEH-k'l-pawst.

1458. General delivery.

פּאָסט־רעסטאַנט·

pawst-res-TAHNT.

1459. Registered.

רעגיסטרירט·

reh-gis-TREERT.

1460. Special delivery.

עקספּרעס·

ex-PRES.

1461. Insured.

פֿאַרזיכערט·

fahr-ZEE-khehrt.

1462. Ten 3 cent stamps.

צען דרײַ־סענטיקע מאַרקעס·

TSEN DRI-SEN-tee-keh MAHR-kes.

1463. I want to send a money order.

איך װיל שיקן אַ פּאָסט־אָנװײַזונג·

eekh VIL SHIK'n ah PAWST-awn-vï-zoongg.

1464. There is nothing dutiable on this.

אױף קײן זאַך אין דעם קומט ניט קײן צאָל·

oyf KAYN ZAHKH in DEM KOOMT nit kayn TSAWL.

1465. Will this go out today?

צי װעט עס נאָך הײַנט אַפּגײן?

tsee vet es nawkh HINT AWP-gayn?

1466. Give me a receipt, please.

גיט מיר אַ קבלה· זײַט אַזױ גוט·

GIT meer ah kah-BAW-leh, ZIT ah-zoy GOOT.

TELEPHONE

1467. Where can I telephone?

װאו קען איך טעלעפֿאָנירן?

VOO KEN eekh teh-leh-faw-NEE-r'n?

1468. Will you telephone for me?

צי קענט איר אָנטעלעפֿאָנירן פֿאַר מיר?

tsee KENT eer AWN-teh-leh-faw-nee-r'n fahr MEER?

1469. I want to make a local call, number ——.

איך װיל קלינגען דאָ הי, נומער ——.

eekh VIL KLIN-gen daw HEE, NOO-mehr ——.

1470. Give me the long distance operator.

גיט מיר די צװישן־שטאַטישע טעלעפֿאָניסטין.

GEET meer dee TSVISH'n-shtaw-tee-sheh teh-leh-faw-NIS-t'n.

1471. The operator will call you.

די טעלעפֿאָניסטין װעט איך אָנקלינגען.

dee teh-leh-faw-NIS-t'n vet ikh 'AWN-klin-gen.

1472. I want number ——.

איך װיל נומער ——.

eekh VIL NOO-mehr ——.

1473. Hello.

האַלאָ.

hah-LAW.

1474. They do not answer.

מען ענטפֿערט ניט.

men ENT-fehrt nit.

1475. The line is busy.

די ליניע איז פֿאַרנומען.

dee LIN-yeh iz fahr-NOO-men.

1476. Hold the line, please.

וואַרט צו, זיט אַזוי גוט·

vahrt TSOO, ZIT ah-zoy GOOT.

1477. May I speak to ——?

צי קען איך רעדן מיט ——?

tsee KEN eekh REH-d'n mit ——?

1478. He is not in.

ער איז ניטאָ·

ehr iz nee-TAW.

1479. This is —— speaking.

דאָס רעדט ——·

daws RET ——.

1480. Please give —— this message.

זיט אַזוי גוט, זאָגט אָן —— אָט וואָס·

ZIT ah-zoy GOOT, zawkt AWN —— AWT vaws.

1481. My number is ——.

מײַן נומער איז ——·

mïn NOO-mehr iz ——.

1482. How much is a call to ——?

וויפֿל קאָסט צו קלינגען קיין ——?

VEE-f'l KAWST tsoo KLIN-gen kayn ——?

1483. There is a telephone call for you.

מען רופֿט איך צום טעלעפֿאָן·

men ROOFT ïkh tsoom teh-leh-FAWN.

TIME AND TIME EXPRESSIONS

1484. What time is it?

וויפֿל האַלט דער זייגער?

VEE-f'l HAHLT dehr ZAY-gehr?

1485. It is two o'clock A.M. (P.M.).

עס איז צוויי אַ זײגער פֿאַר טאָג (נאָך מיטאָג)·

es iz TSVAY ah ZAY-gehr fahr TAWG (nawkh MIT-awg).

1486. It is half past ——.

עס איז האַלב נאָך ——·

es iz HAHLB nawkh ——.

1487. It is quarter past ——.

עס איז אַ פֿערטל נאָך ——·

es iz ah FEHR-t'l nawkh ——.

1488. It is quarter to ——.

עס איז אַ פֿערטל צו ——·

es iz ah FEHR-t'l tsoo ——.

1489. At ten minutes to ——.

צען מינוט צו ——·

TSEN mee-NOOT tsoo ——.

1490. At ten minutes past ——.

צען מינוט נאָך ——·

TSEN mee-NOOT nawkh ——.

1491. In the morning.

אין דער פֿרי·

in dehr FREE.

1492. In the evening.

אין אָוונט·

in AW-v'nt.

1493. In the afternoon.

נאָך מיטאָג·

nawkh MIT-awg.

1494. At noon.

מיטאָגצײַט·

MIT-awg-tsĭt.

1495. Day.
טאָג׳
tawg.

1496. Night.
נאַכט׳
nahkht.

1497. Midnight.
האַלבע נאַכט׳
HAHL-beh NAHKHT.

1498. Yesterday.
נעכטן׳
NEKH-t'n.

1499. Last night.
נעכטן ביי נאַכט׳
NEKH-t'n bī NAHKHT.

1500. Today.
היינט׳
hīnt.

1501. Tonight.
היינט אין אָוונט׳
HĪNT in AW-v'nt.

1502. Tomorrow.
מאָרגן׳
MOR-g'n.

1503. Last year.
פאַר אַ יאָרן׳
fahr ah YAW-r'n.

1504. Last month.
פאַרגאַנגענעם חודש׳
fahr-GAHN-geh-nem KHOY-desh.

1505. Next Monday.

קומענדיקן מאָנטיק׃

KOO-men-dee-k'n MAWN-tik.

1506. Next week.

קומענדיקע װאָך׃

KOO-men-dee-keh VAWKH.

1507. The day before yesterday.

אייער־נעכטן׃

AY-ehr-nekh-t'n.

1508. The day after tomorrow.

איבער מאָרגן׃

EE-behr mor-g'n.

1509. Two weeks ago.

מיט צװיי װאָכן צוריק׃

mit TSVAY VAW-kh'n tsoo-RIK.

1510. One week ago.

פֿאַר אַכט טאָגן׃

fahr ahkht TAW-g'n.

MONTHS

1511. January.

יאַנואַר׃

YAH-noo-ahr.

1512. February.

פֿעברואַר׃

FEB-roo-ahr.

1513. March.

מאַרץ׃

mahrts.

1514. April.
אפריל׃
ahp-RIL.

1515. May.
מײַ׃
mĭ.

1516. June.
יוני׃
YOO-nee.

1517. July.
יולי׃
YOO-lee.

1518. August.
אויגוסט׃
oy-GOOST.

1519. September.
סעפטעמבער׃
sep-TEM-behr.

1520. October.
אָקטאָבער׃
awk-TAW-behr.

1521. November.
נאָװעמבער׃
naw-VEM-behr.

1522. December.
דעצעמבער׃
deh-TSEM-behr.

SEASONS

1523. Spring.
פֿרילינג׃
FREE-lingg.

1524. Summer.

זומער.

ZOO-mehr.

1525. Autumn.

האַרבסט.

hahrbst.

1526. Winter.

ווינטער.

VIN-tehr.

WEATHER

1527. It is warm (cold).

עס איז וואַרעם (קאַלט).

es iz VAH-rem (KAHLT).

1528. It is fair (good, bad).

עס איז שיין (גוט, שלעכט).

es iz SHAYN (GOOT, SHLEKHT).

1529. It is raining (snowing).

עס רעגנט (שנייט).

es REH-g'nt (SHNAYT).

1530. The sun.

די זון.

dee ZOON.

1531. Sunny.

זוניק.

ZOO-nik.

1532. The shade.

דער שאָטן.

dehr SHAW-t'n.

DAYS OF THE WEEK

1533. Sunday.
זונטיק.
ZOON-tik.

1534. Monday.
מאָנטיק.
MAWN-tik.

1535. Tuesday.
דינסטיק.
DEENS-tik.

1536. Wednesday.
מיטוואָך.
MIT-vawkh.

1537. Thursday.
דאָנערשטיק.
DAW-nehrsh-tik.

1538. Friday.
פֿרײַטיק.
FRI-tik.

1539. Saturday.
שבת.
SHAH-bes.

HOLIDAYS

1540. Rosh Hashanah.
ראָש־השנה.
raw-sheh-SHAW-neh.

1541. Yom Kippur.
יום־כּיפּור.
yin-KIP-ehr.

1542. Sukkoth.
סוכּות.
SOO-kes.

1543. Channukah.
חנוכּה.
KHAH-nee-keh.

1544. Purim.
פּורים.
POO-rim.

1545. Passover.
פּסח.
PAY-sahkh.

1546. Shevuoth.
שבועות.
SHVOO-es.

1547. Legal holiday.
אָפֿיציעלער יום־טוב.
aw-fits-YEH-lehr YAWN-tev.

1548. New year's.
ניַ־יאָר.
NI-yawr.

1549. Easter.
פּאַסכע.
PAHS-kheh.

1550. Christmas.
ניטל.
NIT'l.

NUMBERS: CARDINALS

1551. 1. One.
אײנס.
ayns.

    2. Two.
צווײ.
tsvay.

3. **Three.**

דריי.

dri .

4. **Four.**

פיר.

feer.

5. **Five.**

פינף.

finf.

6. **Six.**

זעקס.

zex.

7. **Seven.**

זיבן.

ZIB'n.

8. **Eight.**

אכט.

ahkht.

9. **Nine.**

ניין.

nin.

10. **Ten.**

צען.

tsen.

11. **Eleven.**

עלף.

elf.

12. **Twelve.**

צוועלף.

tsvelf.

13. **Thirteen.**

דרייצן.

DRI-ts'n.

14. **Fourteen.**

פערצן.

FEHR-ts'n.

15. Fifteen.
פופֿצן·
FOOF-ts'n.

16. Sixteen.
זעכצן·
ZEKH-ts'n.

17. Seventeen.
זיבעצן·
ZIB-eh-ts'n.

18. Eighteen.
אכצן·
AHKH-ts'n.

19. Nineteen.
נײַנצן·
NIN-ts'n.

20. Twenty.
צוואַנציק·
TSVAHN-tsik.

21. Twenty-one.
אײן און צוואַנציק·
AYN oon TSVAHN-tsik.

22. Twenty-two.
צוויי און צוואַנציק·
TSVAY oon TSVAHN-tsik.

30. Thirty.
דרײַסיק·
DRI-sik.

40. Forty.
פֿערציק·
FEHR-tsik.

50. Fifty.
פופֿציק·
FOOF-tsik.

60. Sixty.
זעכציק·
ZEKH-tsik.

70. Seventy.
זיבעציק·
ZIB-eh-tsik.

80. Eighty.
אַכציק·
AHKH-tsik.

90. Ninety
נײנציק·
NINE-tsik.

100. One hundred.
הונדערט·
HOON-dehrt.

200. Two hundred.
צוויי הונדערט·
TSVAY hoon-dehrt.

1000. One thousand.
טויזנט·
TOY-z'nt.

2000. Two thousand.
צוויי טויזנט·
TSVAY TOY-z'nt.

1958.
נײנצן אַכט און פופציק·
NIN-ts'n AHKHT oon FOOF-tsik.

NUMBERS: ORDINALS

1552. First.
ערשטער·
EHR-shtehr.

Second.
צווייטער·
TSVAY-tehr.

Third.
דריטער·
DRIT-ehr.

Fourth.

פֿערטער׳

FEHR-tehr.

Fifth.

פֿינפֿטער׳

FINF-tehr.

Sixth.

זעקסטער׳

ZEKS-tehr.

Seventh.

זיבעטער׳

ZIB-eh-tehr.

Eighth.

אַכטער׳

AHKH-tehr.

Ninth.

נײַנטער׳

NIN-tehr.

Tenth.

צענטער׳

TSEN-tehr.

USEFUL ARTICLES

1553. The ash tray.

דאָס אַשטעצל׳

daws AHSH-teh-ts'l.

1554. The bobby pins.

די האָרנאָדלען׳

dee HAWR-nawd-len.

1555. The bottle opener.

דער פֿלאַש־עפֿענער׳

dehr FLAHSH-eh-feh-nehr.

1556. The box.

דאָס קעסטל׳

daws KES-t'l.

1557. The bulb (light).

דאָס לעמפּל•

daws LEM-p'l.

1558. The candy.

די צוקערקע•

dee tsoo-KEHR-keh.

1559. The can opener.

דער קאָנסערוון־עפֿענער•

dehr kawn- SEHR-v'n-eh-feh-nehr.

1560. The cleaning fluid.

די רייניק־פֿליסיקייט•

dee RAY-nik-flee-see-kit.

1561. The cloth.

די טוך•

dee TOOKH.

1562. The clock.

דער זייגער•

dehr ZAY-gehr.

1563. The cork.

דער קאָריק•

dehr KAW-rik.

1564. The corkscrew.

דער קאָריק־ציער•

dehr KAW-rik-tsee-ehr.

1565. The cushion.

דער קישן•

dehr KEE-sh'n.

1566. The doll.

די ליאַלקע•

dee LAHL-keh.

1567. A pair of earrings.

אַ פּאָר אוירינגלעך•

ah pawr OY-ringg-lekh.

1568. The flashlight.

דאָס באַטעריע־לעמפּל•

daws bah-TEHR-yeh-lem-p'l.

1569. The sunglasses.

די זונברילן∙

dee ZOON-bri-l'n.

1570. The gold.

דאָס גאָלד∙

daws GAWLD.

1571. The chewing gum.

די קײגומע∙

dee KI-goo-meh.

1572. The hairnet.

די האָרנעץ∙

dee HAWR-nets.

1573. The hooks.

די העקלעך∙

dee HEK-lekh.

1574. The jewelry.

די צירונג∙

dee TSEE-roongg.

1575. The leather.

די לעדער∙

dee LEH-dehr.

1576. The linen.

דאָס ליוונט∙

daws LI-v'nt.

1577. The lock.

דער שלאָס∙

dehr SHLAWS.

1578. The mirror.

דער שפּיגל∙

dehr SHPEE-g'l.

1579. The mosquito net.

די קאָמאַרן-נעץ∙

dee kow-MAH-r'n-nets.

1580. The necklace.

די האַלדזבאַנד∙

dee HAHLDZ-bahnd.

1581. The needle.

די נאָדל.

dee NAW-d'l.

1582. The notebook.

די העפֿט.

dee HEFT.

1583. The pail.

דער עמער.

dehr EH-mehr.

1584. The penknife.

דאָס מעסערל.

daws MEH-seh-r'l.

1585. The perfume.

די פּאַרפֿום.

dee pahr-FOOM.

1586. The pin (ornamental).

די בראָש.

dee BRAWSH.

1587. The pin (safety).

די זיכער־נאָדל.

dee ZEE-khehr-naw-d'l.

1588. The pin (straight).

די שפּילקע.

dee SHPIL-keh.

1589. The purse.

דער בײַטל.

dehr BI-t'l.

1590. The radio.

דער ראַדיאָ.

dehr RAHD-yaw.

1591. The ring.

דאָס פֿינגערל.

daws FIN-geh-r'l.

1592. A pair of rubbers.

אַ פּאָר קאַלאָשן.

ah pawr kah-LAW-sh'n.

1593. The scissors.
די שער־
dee SHEHR.

1594. The screw.
דער שרויף־
dehr SHROYF.

1595. A pair of shoelaces.
א פאר שוכבענדלעך־
ah pawr SHOOKH-bend-lekh.

1596. The silk.
דאָס זייד־
daws ZID.

1597. The silver.
דאָס זילבער־
daws ZIL-behr.

1598. The (precious) stone.
דער (איידעלער) שטיין־
dehr (AY-deh-lehr) SHTAYN.

1599. The stopper.
דאָס פאָרשטעקל־
daws fahr-SHTEH-k'l.

1600. The suitcase.
דער טשעמאָדאַן־
dehr cheh-maw-DAHN.

1601. The thimble.
דער פינגערהוט־
dehr FIN-gehr-hoot.

1602. The thread.
דער פאָדעם־
dehr FAW-dem.

1603. The typewriter.
די שרײבמאַשין־
dee SHRIB-mah-sheen.

1604. The umbrella.
דער שירעם־
dehr SHEE-rem.

1605. The vase.

די וואַזע∙

dee VAH-zeh.

1606. The watch.

דער זייגער∙

dehr ZAY-gehr.

1607. The whiskbroom.

די קליידערבאַרשט∙

dee KLAY-dehr-bahrsht.

1608. The wire.

דער דראָט∙

dehr DRAWT.

1609. The wood.

דאָס האָלץ∙

daws HAWLTS.

1610. The wool.

די וואָל∙

dee VAWL.

1611. The zipper.

דאָס בליצשלעסל∙

daws BLITS-shleh-s'l.

INDEX

All the sentences, phrases and words in this book are numbered consecutively from 1–1611. The numbers in the index refer to these entries. In addition, each major section (capitalized) is indexed according to *page number*.

LISTEN & LEARN CASSETTES

Complete, practical at-home language learning courses for people with limited study time—specially designed for travelers.

Special features:

• Dual-language—Each phrase first in English, then the foreign-language equivalent, followed by a pause for repetition (allows for easy use of cassette even without manual).

• Native speakers—Spoken by natives of the country who are language teachers at leading colleges and universities.

• Convenient manual—Contains every word on the cassettes—all fully indexed for fast phrase or word location.

Each boxed set contains one 90-minute cassette and complete manual.

Listen & Learn French . . . . .Cassette and Manual
99914-9 $9.95

Listen & Learn German . . . . . . .Cassette and Manual
99915-7 $9.95

Listen & Learn Italian . . . . .Cassette and Manual
99916-5 $9.95

Listen & Learn Japanese . . . . . . .Cassette and Manual
99917-3 $9.95

Listen & Learn Modern Greek . .Cassette and Manual
99921-1 $9.95

Listen & Learn Modern Hebrew Cassette and Manual
99923-8 $9.95

Listen & Learn Russian . . . . .Cassette and Manual
99920-3 $9.95

Listen & Learn Spanish . . . . .Cassette and Manual
99918-1 $9.95

Listen & Learn Swedish . . . . .Cassette and Manual
99922-X $9.95

Precise, to-the-point guides for adults with limited learning time

ESSENTIAL GRAMMAR SERIES

Designed for independent study or as supplements to conventional courses, the *Essential Grammar* series provides clear explanations of all aspects of grammar—no trivia, no archaic material. Do not confuse these volumes with abridged grammars. These volumes are complete. All volumes 5⅜" x 8½".

ESSENTIAL FRENCH GRAMMAR, Seymour Resnick. 159pp.   °20419-7 Pa. $4.95

ESSENTIAL GERMAN GRAMMAR, Guy Stern and E. F. Bleiler. 124pp.   °20422-7 Pa. $4.95

ESSENTIAL ITALIAN GRAMMAR, Olga Ragusa. 111pp.
°20779-X Pa. $4.95

ESSENTIAL JAPANESE GRAMMAR, E. F. Bleiler. 156pp.
21027-8 Pa. $5.95

ESSENTIAL PORTUGUESE GRAMMAR, Alexander da R. Prista. 114pp.   21650-0 Pa. $5.95

ESSENTIAL SPANISH GRAMMAR, Seymour Resnick. 115pp.
°20780-3 Pa. $4.95

ESSENTIAL MODERN GREEK GRAMMAR, Douglas Q. Adams. 128pp.   25133-0 Pa. $5.95

ESSENTIAL DUTCH GRAMMAR, Henry R. Stern. 110pp.
24675-2 Pa. $5.95

ESSENTIAL ENGLISH GRAMMAR, Philip Gucker. 177pp.
21649-7 Pa. $4.95

°Not available in British Commonwealth Countries except Canada.